No Better Time

No Better Time

*The Brief, Remarkable Life
of Danny Lewin—
The Genius Who
Transformed the Internet*

Molly Knight Raskin

DA CAPO PRESS
A Member of the Perseus Books Group

Da Capo Press
A Member of the Perseus Books Group

Copyright © 2013 by Molly Knight Raskin

Printed in the United States of America.

For information, address Da Capo Press, 44 Farnsworth Street, 3rd Floor,
Boston, MA 02210.

Cataloging-in-Publication data for this book is available from the Library of
Congress.
First Da Capo Press edition 2013
ISBN: 978-0-306-82166-0 (hardcover)
ISBN: 978-0-306-82167-7 (e-book)

Published by Da Capo Press
A Member of the Perseus Books Group
www.dacapopress.com

Da Capo Press books are available at special discounts for bulk purchases in the
U.S. by corporations, institutions, and other organizations. For more
information, please contact the Special Markets Department at the Perseus
Books Group, 2300 Chestnut Street, Suite 200, Philadelphia, PA, 19103, or call
(800) 810-4145, ext. 5000, or e-mail special.markets@perseusbooks.com.

10 9 8 7 6 5 4 3 2 1

Dedicated to Matt, Sophie, & Claire

Contents

"An algorithm must be seen to be believed."

—DONALD KNUTH,
The Art of Computer Programming

Preface

In the spring of 2011, a friend asked if I was interested in a job co-producing an independent film tribute for the anniversary of the 9/11 attacks. The subject, he explained, was a passenger on the first plane to crash into the North Tower of the World Trade Center. From there, the story took on a life of its own.

It is the story of Daniel "Danny" Mark Lewin (1970–2001), who was almost certainly the first victim of the 9/11 attacks. It's the story of an extraordinarily gifted young man who believed anything was possible and let nothing stand in his way. Of an all-American kid who moved to Israel against his will, ended up falling hopelessly in love with the country, and served as an officer in the most elite unit of the Israeli army. Of a young soldier who was trained to hunt and kill terrorists, and who—in a tragic twist of irony—later died at their hands. Of a loud, irreverent young computer science student who formed a beautiful friendship with a soft-spoken, reserved professor. Of a husband and father who spent years struggling to make ends meet and became a billionaire almost overnight. Of a theoretical mathematician who wrote a set of algorithms that would change the Internet forever.

Until now, it's also a story that has remained largely untold. When Lewin was still alive, business journalists categorized him and his company, Akamai, as breakout stars of the first dot-com boom. After his death on 9/11, the mainstream media eulogized him as one of the 2,975 victims of the attacks but never fully investigated his actions on American Airlines Flight 11. His family and friends have remained largely silent. They are certain Lewin courageously tried to stop the terrorists, and that he was likely the first victim of the attacks, but they have been reluctant to share publicly why they believe this to be fact.

Some stories, I have learned, simply can't be told without the passage of time. You can dig at them, push them, pound the pavement in search of ways to bring them to life, but you can't be true to them until their keepers are ready to share a part of their lives long shrouded in privacy. It's not until that point that they will reach willingly into the wells of their memory, perhaps even back to those moments hardest to relive, and begin to tell the story.

CHAPTER 1

World Wide Wait

"If people do not believe that mathematics is simple, it is only because they do not realize how complicated life is."

—JOHN VON NEUMANN,
1947, first national meeting of the Association
for Computing Machinery

In the fall of 1996, a graduate student at the Massachusetts Institute of Technology came crashing into the quiet, cramped office of Professor Frank Thomson "Tom" Leighton with a tsunami-like enthusiasm. His name was Daniel "Danny" Lewin. Leighton distinctly remembered the favorable impression he formed of the energetic young student from Israel.

Leighton was not easy to impress—at least not in an academic setting. As a professor at MIT for more than a decade, he spent most of his days in the company of greatness. Leighton and his colleagues at MIT's Laboratory for Computer Science (LCS)* were legends in their field whose collective contributions read like a laundry list of computing and mathematical breakthroughs of the twentieth century. If you were one of the privileged handful of students accepted into the program each year, you quickly faced the fact that, at LCS, brilliance alone wasn't rewarded; it was assumed.

Over the years, Leighton witnessed a steady host of students—most of them serious, industrious whiz kids—cycle through LCS. Leighton enjoyed working with them, excited by each new class and the possibility that, through his lectures or research projects, he might fan some spark in their nascent minds. But for Leighton, the most exciting possibility of all was this: the opportunity to work with a student smart and inspired enough to push Leighton himself beyond the boundaries of his own scientific pursuits. These kinds of

---

*In 2003, MIT's Laboratory for Computer Science (LCS) merged with the Artificial Intelligence (AI) Lab to form the MIT Computer Science and Artificial Intelligence Laboratory, or CSAIL.

students are statistical rarities, and Leighton was always on the look-out for them.

The semester of 1996 began like most at MIT, with thousands of students descending onto the university's sprawling urban campus on the Charles River, directly across from Boston. They came from all over, the best and brightest minds drawn to MIT for its culture of cutting edge research and rigorous scientific inquiry. Churning out patent applications and spawning companies at an astounding rate, MIT has long been synonymous with the spirit of innovation. Founded in 1916 to serve the needs of a new industrial age, MIT quickly became one of the top research institutions in the world, and it still is today. And when it comes to computer science, MIT is almost unrivaled, consistently ranked as the first or second (to Stanford University or Carnegie Mellon) in the nation.

Lewin arrived in Cambridge late that summer on his own, leaving his wife, Anne, and two sons—Eitan and Itamar, a newborn—to remain in Israel until he settled into their new apartment. Lewin was American, born and raised in a suburb of Denver, Colorado. But he spent most of his formative years in Israel, moving there at age fourteen and attending a Hebrew high school. After graduating at age eighteen, he joined the Israel Defense Forces (IDF) and served almost four years, after which he attended college at the Israel Institute of Technology (the Technion) in Haifa. For Lewin, Israel was home, and moving back to America wasn't easy. When he landed in Boston on a flight from Tel Aviv with little more than a few suitcases, Lewin experienced a bout of culture shock. The city was chilly, and he had nothing warmer than a fleece jacket in his wardrobe. His assigned apartment, located in a graduate housing complex near campus, was more modest than he expected, small for a family of four and their belongings. But as a former officer in one of the most elite units of the IDF, Lewin was quick to adapt. He set out to make Cambridge home and join the ranks of another elite cadre—LCS.

He was immediately assigned to Professor Leighton (first as his teaching assistant, then as his research assistant), who was at that time head of the algorithms group at LCS.

Leighton soon found himself looking forward to Lewin's visits, which punctuated his typically quiet, serious academic life with bursts of exuberance. And it wasn't just the student's gusto that intrigued Leighton. When he spoke about topics that energized him, which seemed to include almost everything, Lewin became so animated—arms gesticulating, eyes ablaze—that his enthusiasm was infectious. "He definitely wasn't the shy, retiring type," Leighton recalled. "What stood out to me was how engaging he was, almost like this live wire. When Danny was excited about something, you couldn't help but get excited, too." Like any incoming student eager to establish himself, Lewin not only dropped by Leighton's office to pick up stacks of student papers to grade but also typically lingered long enough to strike up a conversation. "We started talking about research problems," explained Leighton. "That's when he began to really distinguish himself, because he had such smart things to say."

In some ways, Lewin's appearance belied his intelligence. Lacking the physical traits of the stereotypical mathematician, he could have easily been mistaken for a high school athlete. Although he stood just five feet ten inches tall, Lewin was built like a bull—burly and broad-shouldered, sheer muscle from head to toe. He was boyishly handsome, with a soft, round face, blue eyes and brown hair that was prematurely receding, giving way to a long, smooth forehead. His smile was unyielding and almost impish, creating in those around him the urge to smile, too. In contrast to the quiet shuffle of most students across MIT's campus, Lewin moved with a distinctive spring in his step, as if he were in a hurry to get somewhere.

In the cluttered, unkempt halls of LCS, over desks piled high with papers and textbooks, or crossing the campus quads, Lewin and Leighton spent hours absorbed in mind-bending conversations about math and computer science. "I felt like I was talking to an equal," recalled Leighton. "He'd think of clever ways to take an idea in some new direction. That's the best kind of research activity; it's rewarding, enjoyable and just a lot of fun." Lewin joined Leighton's algorithms group, which was grappling with a challenging set of problems centered on this new mode of communication, the Internet, and some of the barriers to its growth.

At the time, neither Leighton nor Lewin could have predicted just how greatly the ground beneath them was beginning to shift with the stirrings of the dot-com boom.

While the Internet as we know it today was conceived as a collaboration between government, academic, and private sectors, its creation began in earnest at MIT in the 1960s. Over the course of the decade, a close-knit community of engineers and scientists worked in relative anonymity to develop the underpinnings of a vast computer network. These "fathers" of the Internet shared the belief that technology and humanity were inextricably linked, foreseeing a time when we would have the connective power of this electronic network at our fingertips. It was a revolutionary idea for a time when computers were expensive, colossal, calculating machines. One of the Internet's earliest proponents was a mild-mannered Midwesterner, Joseph Carl Robnett Licklider. Known as J. C. R. or "Lick" to friends, Licklider—a preeminent Harvard psychologist-turned-MIT computer scientist—wrote a series of essays in the early 1960s documenting his vision for a globally interactive set of computers.

Around the same time, graduate student Leonard Kleinrock—a fast-talking kid from the Bronx on a full scholarship at MIT—was deep into his doctoral thesis on how to stabilize and increase the flow of information within this hypothetical network of computers. Kleinrock knew that the system of circuits used to transmit a telephone call, which has a centralized point of control, would not function well when moving large amounts of data between computer networks. His solution, which he outlined in his thesis, was a clever theory called "packet switching."* Simply put, packet switching involves the breaking apart of data into separate, small blocks, each one tagged with an address. When the information blocks reach their destination, the network reassembles them. Packet switching later became one of the Internet's fundamental networking technologies.[1]

This flurry of research at MIT gave rise to Project Mathematics and Computation (or Project MAC), which took off in the summer of 1963 with a $2 million grant from the Department of Defense for the development of a robust, fault-tolerant computer network. Under the leadership of Licklider, the Project MAC team immediately began building a large-scale network of computers called AR-PANET, the precursor to the Internet.

The work on ARPANET was unusually collaborative; the Project MAC team joined forces with commercial computer companies such as Bolt, Beranek and Newman (BBN) to get the network off the ground. A computer at UCLA became the first "node" or point of connection for ARPANET. By December 1969, three more nodes had been added at the Stanford Research Institute (SRI), UC Santa Barbara, and the University of Utah, establishing a four-node network. As ARPANET grew in size and scope, so did the number of key players involved in its success. One of them was Vinton Cerf, who later became vice president and "chief Internet evangelist" of Google. With a PhD in computer science from UCLA, Cerf spent several years working directly with Robert Khan, an applied mathematician and computer scientist at MIT and BBN, to develop a "virtual

---

*A number of scientists pioneered aspects of packet switching, including Paul Baran at Rand Corporation, who developed the architecture of packet networks, and Donald Davies at England's National Physics Laboratory, who coined the term "packet."

handshake" (Transmission Control Protocol/Internet Protocol, or TCP/IP) that allowed computers in disparate places to talk to one another.[2]

By 1990 ARPANET had been decommissioned to make way for a much broader network supported by the National Science Foundation, and a growing number of commercial Internet Service Providers (ISPs). A year later, Al Gore—then a young senator from Tennessee—paved the way for the information superhighway by steering a bill through Congress that supported the creation of the Internet beyond academic and scientific institutions. The Internet had fully evolved from an academic experiment in shared intelligence into an explosive commercial enterprise.

Because of the time, there was even more of a buzz in the air than usual when Danny Lewin joined MIT's LCS in the fall of 1996. By the mid-1990s, the lab was not only at the forefront of computing; it was also on the frontlines of the burgeoning dot-com boom. Under the leadership of Michael Dertouzos, formerly a computer scientist with Project MAC, LCS remained a hive of innovation. It inspired dozens of tech companies, including 3Com, a multibillion-dollar networking business co-founded by computer scientist Robert Metcalfe, and RSA Data Security, led by Ron Rivest, the inventor of the public-key encryption that allows us to securely enter information like credit card numbers online. LCS was also home to the World Wide Web Consortium (W3C), the Web's international standards organization created by British computer scientist Tim Berners-Lee.

If Silicon Valley was the heart of the dot-com boom, Cambridge was its intellectual capital. The combined talent of the city's crown jewels, MIT and Harvard, helped transform Cambridge from a biotech center into an incubator for the digital age. Clusters of startups with names like Frictionless and Viant rose out of its labs, offices, and dormitories. The greater Boston area was second only to Northern California in the number of computer companies that called it home. By the mid-1990s, 1,500 software companies had taken up shop in Cambridge and its surrounding areas.[3]

Ironically, the high-tech activity had little to no bearing on Lewin's decision to attend MIT. Having been accepted to every one of the top ten graduate programs in computer science, he had had his pick of schools—Cal Tech, Stanford, and Carnegie Mellon, to name a few. Some even wooed him with generous scholarships. With the rigor of a mathematician, Lewin drew up a list, annotating it with the pros and cons of each school. The verdict wasn't all his to determine, of course. He had a family to consider, and Anne was excited by the idea of moving to a sun-drenched campus in California. For Lewin, however, the decision had, in some ways, already been made.

Lewin had MIT in his sights as early as 1986, when he was just a teenager otherwise preoccupied with pretty girls. That September, he wrote a letter to his best friend, Marco Greenberg, in the U.S. In it, he told Greenberg he was trying to study for the *bagrats* (Israeli matriculation exams), but that flirtatious girls were distracting him. "The girls in school are trying the 'FIRST STRIKE' technique on me," Lewin wrote, adding, "This is a very good opening to the school year!!!" It was a typical teenage letter, until page three, when Lewin casually noted: "If I graduate this year, I'll go back for school. I don't know where, but I would love any of the technical schools, [e.g.] MIT." Lewin's mention of MIT was one of several hints that tipped Greenberg off to his friend's higher-than-average intelligence. A few years later, while the two were talking about college, Greenberg mentioned that, if Lewin wanted to go to an American school, he would have to complete the SAT (Standardized Aptitude Test). Much to Greenberg's surprise, Lewin told him that he'd already taken the exam—for fun. When Greenberg pressed him about his scores, Lewin matter-of-factly answered: near perfect on the English, and perfect on the math.

Engineers built the hardware for computers and the Internet, computer scientists programmed the machines, and entrepreneurs forged new businesses on the vast new landscape. But nowhere in this developing ecosystem could one find a clearly defined role for the theoretical computer scientist.

In the 1990s, computer science was still a relatively new discipline. Naturally, the mathematical subset of this field, theoretical computer science (TCS), was even more novel and arcane. In part, its complexity was the cause, and it still is today. When you ask theoretical computer scientists to explain what, exactly, they do for a living, the answer is often too lofty for the average mind to grasp. Take, for example, Professor Leighton's puzzling description of his early work at MIT: "I was interested in properties of networks and how to send messages through them. I wasn't writing code, instead I was using math. So I'd say, for example, that if the network has N nodes, and every node needs to send a message to another node, there's a way of routing all the messages so they don't collide and they all get to their destinations at the same amount of time. If your problem is size N, where N is a variable, it will take some function of N, like 10 n."

Leighton earned his PhD in math from MIT in 1981 and became a professor the next year. By the late 1980s, he was leading the theory group at LCS, the largest of its kind in the world, becoming somewhat of a celebrity in the rarefied field. TCS sits at the intersection between math and computation and relies heavily on algorithms, which are step-by-step procedures for calculations. Characterized by abstraction and complex ideas, TCS has long been relegated to a lesser status than other areas of computer science. If you're a theoretician, then it's often assumed you can't also be an applied scientist. And if you're not an applied scientist, then you're not coming up with practical solutions. As Leighton writes in a paper examining the merits of his field:

> TCS researchers create mathematical models, rely on abstractions, and establish facts using proofs. They seek to answer questions such as how long an algorithm takes to run, what resources it requires, and how much noise it can tolerate—but they obtain answers through analysis, instead of conjecture or simulation.

Over time, theoretical computer scientists have, in fact, made extraordinary contributions to the world. At MIT, one of the most celebrated inventions is public key encryption, created by professors Ron Rivest, Adi Shamir, and Leonard Aldeman. Developing what's called the RSA algorithm, the three scientists came up with the system that now facilitates almost all online e-commerce, financial transactions, and secure Web site logins. Another MIT graduate, electrical engineer Andrew James Viterbi, is responsible for the invention of the Viterbi algorithm. At first, the algorithm was seen as nothing more than a beautiful theory. But eventually, with advancements in hardware technology, the value of Viterbi's decoding algorithms became clear and they are now used in billions of cell phones and digital television sets around the world. Viterbi left MIT to co-found Qualcomm, the telecommunications giant, and is now a professor at the University of Southern California's engineering school founded in his name.

Despite these achievements, TCS was, and still is, relegated to a lower rank at universities around the country, mainly because its foundations remain abstract to all but a small minority, and it's not the biggest catalyst of tangible, real-world results. "Back then, theory was at the bottom of the totem pole," recalled Leighton. "It's better now, but back then we were like the weak sister." As a consequence, when it came to funding the research pioneering the Internet, TCS was never top of the list. Somehow Leighton still managed to secure government research funds in the late 1980s to explore ways to route and store data on the Internet from a mathematical perspective. But he was mostly on his own: "I was the token mathematician," Leighton said. "I don't think anyone was looking to me, or my group, for anything groundbreaking." Leighton's own research centered on parallel algorithms and architectures. So little was known about this area of computer science that it had not even been covered in textbooks. Leighton set out to write one, and it took him the better part of seven years. Published in 1992, the hefty, 831-page *Introduction to Parallel Algorithms and Architectures: Arrays, Trees, Hypercubes* became a seminal text in computer science.

By his late thirties, Leighton had reached an enviable place in life. He was a tenured professor at MIT and one of the world's preeminent authorities on algorithms for computing. Academia was his lifeblood, and his research garnered him a wide array of prestigious accolades, including the Machty Award and the National Science Foundation's Young Investigator Award. Occasionally, he even turned a profit outside of MIT by patenting his ideas. One idea, which he sold to Polaroid, is still used to create the 2-D barcode on the back of drivers' licenses.

Leighton married Bonnie Berger, also a professor at LCS and a renowned expert in randomized algorithms. A petite woman with large brown eyes and the industrious energy of excessive brainpower, Berger was the first female in MIT's math department to earn tenure. She and Leighton met at an MIT party before Berger began graduate work at the university, and Berger said she knew almost instantly he was the man she wanted to marry. It was not until a decade later that they became engaged. Berger still remembered her mother's response to the news that her daughter was settling down with a math professor. "My mother said to keep in mind that I was marrying a math professor and my life would not be up to the standards that I was accustomed to," she recounted. Leighton and Berger had a son, Alexander. They lived in a beautiful home outside Cambridge and worked in offices across the hall from one another in MIT's Tech Square building.

Leighton was, and still is, full of quiet ambition. But the mid-90s, when Danny Lewin arrived at MIT, Leighton was also keenly aware that he'd worked long and hard to reach a point at which he was challenged yet also content. "I could have solved proofs all day that no one would ever read," Leighton admitted. "And I would have been happy doing that."

Tom Leighton was Lewin's one and only mentor at MIT, but he wasn't the first professor to earn the unflagging admiration of the eager young computer scientist. At the Israel Institute of Technology (Technion), Professor Alfred "Freddy" Bruckstein, who taught electrical engineering and computer science for nearly a decade, remembered clearly the fall of 1992, when Lewin arrived in his office in much the same way he greeted Leighton years later. Lewin, an undergraduate, was not one of Bruckstein's students, but he came bursting in one day excited to discuss one of the professor's most challenging areas of interest: knot theory.

"His brightness was a given, but it was his enthusiasm that I remember the most," explained Bruckstein, who today serves as the Ollendorff Chair of Science at the Technion. "His eyes were scintillating. He was immersed, interested, and had this fantastic drive."

Bruckstein was working to develop software that he could use to program robots to manipulate knots flexibly. According to Bruckstein, the problem was easy to state but extremely difficult to solve using math. Unlike the frustration he saw in countless other students grappling with unwieldy science, Bruckstein saw nothing but enjoyment in Lewin. "Knots are complex, and he loved them," Bruckstein related. "In fact, I think he loved them for their complexity."

An award-winning computer scientist and mathematician, Bruckstein was, and remains, the consummate professor. He wakes up in the mornings looking forward to hours immersed in labs or textbooks. Bruckstein's research has always focused on quirky mathematics, robotics, and imaging. He has studied the response of movement-sensing neurons in the eyes of a fly and has created a mathematical model to analyze the perfectly straight trails of ants marching in pursuit of food. Eccentric to some, to Lewin these studies were captivating.

Like the majority of students at the Technion, Lewin was searching for a topic for his first paper. He proposed to Bruckstein a project that would use algorithms to program robots working with knots. Bruckstein didn't expect much in the way of results from a first-year student, but he was so taken with Lewin that he approved the project, sending him off with some words of encouragement. Lewin spent several weeks working on the paper with another student, friend Orli Gann. When they delivered their paper, titled "Trivial or Knot," to Bruckstein, he was so impressed that he encouraged them to publish their results. "It was a beautiful project, and I didn't expect to get such nicely documented results," said Bruckstein, who still uses the software today.

Over the next few years, Freddy Bruckstein and Danny Lewin became friends. Although Bruckstein, at age thirty-eight, was fifteen years older than Lewin, they could talk endlessly about science, politics, and life. Bruckstein and his family lived in the apartment building directly next door to Danny, Anne, and their first son, Eitan. Bruckstein's son, Ariel, played often with Eitan in the small park outside their apartment complex. Bruckstein recalled feeling a sense of sadness when, in July of 1996, Lewin handed him a letter stating that he would be leaving the Technion, where he had planned to pursue a PhD, to attend MIT. Bruckstein said he was sorry to bid farewell to a dear friend, but he was comforted by Lewin's hope to return one day to teach at the Technion. He was also filled with pride: "I told him to go, of course. MIT is top of the world."

At MIT, Lewin found a new mentor in Tom Leighton. And Leighton found a cerebral match and enthusiastic collaborator in Lewin. An intellectual courtship began. Leighton and Lewin were both fluent in the language of mathematics, a precise vernacular punctuated by statements such as if/then and true/false. The two of them would toss ideas back and forth, elaborating on the most exciting ones until those concepts took on lives of their own. The brainstorming, Leighton said, became both conscious and subconscious. Oftentimes, ideas made their way into his dreams, jolting him out of sleep at odd hours. The same was true for Lewin, who was known to fire off lengthy, thoughtful e-mail missives in the middle of the night. "It's like working on a crossword puzzle; you get stuck and you put it away," Leighton clarified. "Then you won't think about it for a while and suddenly—bang! You have the answer, because the brain works even though you're not aware of it. That's what happens with math."

With Lewin in lock step, Leighton's life began to move just a bit faster. Even Bonnie Berger said she couldn't help but poke her head in her husband's office when she heard Lewin stop by. "It was quite a circus when Danny arrived," recalled Berger. "He just was the most energetic force that you could imagine; it was hard to ignore. I'd come in and listen, and he would be jumping around the whiteboard with this muscular, physical power."

The more Lewin got to know Leighton, the more professionally enamored he became, routinely telling friends he'd met the "smartest man in the world." Leighton was also incredibly nice, which impressed Lewin, who had no tolerance for self-importance. Genteel and soft-spoken, Leighton had none of the airs of an ivory tower professor.

And yet they were an unlikely pair, the professor and the student. More than ten years Lewin's senior, Leighton was calm and measured, in sharp contrast to Lewin's fiery, often impetuous nature. Even in physical appearance, they were an unusual duo. Leighton was lean and serious looking, with prematurely graying hair, piercing blue eyes and the ramrod straight posture of an admiral. Lewin was strong and stocky, with the burly physique of a soldier. They spent the bulk of their time together, rarely disagreeing. "They were just such a good match," Berger confirmed. "They were both really smart, and Tom totally appreciated Danny. I also think Tom was a calming influence. Danny was young and impulsive at times, and Tom would say, 'What are you thinking?' I also think they were an amazing pair because they both completely trusted each other."

Leighton was reserved but possessed of steadfast determination. Lewin was unabashedly outspoken and indomitable. Both of them were drawn, in their own ways, to the toughest problems facing their field.

It's hard to imagine from the vantage point of today's hyper-wired world, but going online in the late 1990s meant cranking up a modem and waiting an average of twenty seconds as it chirped and beeped, straining to connect with the seemingly magical, futuristic world of cyberspace. In 1996, only twenty million Americans had access to the Internet. For most people, it remained a source of fascination and bewilderment. As the largest Internet Service Provider (ISP) at the time, America Online (AOL) led the pack with five million subscribers. AOL also had the most popular Web site, AOL.

com, by virtue of the fact that when its members dialed into the Web, they were immediately directed to the company's home page. That summer marked the launch of the first webmail site, Hotmail, but there was no instant messaging or music trading. No streaming music or video. The question on most people's minds was how, exactly, could the Internet be used? It was the new American frontier.[4]

At the time, the Internet functioned fairly well within small communities like academic institutions, but, otherwise, it remained seriously flawed. A common scenario in those days involved a user who dialed into the Internet using a home telephone line, which allowed him or her to access information at speeds of only tens of kilobytes per second, compared with tens of megabytes today (more than a tenfold increase). These wait times were frustrating, arising mainly because a server—the powerful computer that responds to requests for information—could be sitting anywhere in the country and it took time for the information stream to move.

The root of the problem lay in the Internet's architecture, originally designed like highways connected by various tunnels, or a "network of networks." The inner workings of this architecture are highly technical and complex, but a basic understanding of how the Web works is surprisingly easy using a familiar analogy: the Pony Express.

When you click on a Web link, think of it as the act of dispatching a rider from your browser to a storage facility known as a web server. The first thing the rider has to do is figure out where the storage facility is. To get the address, the rider consults the Internet address book, also known as the Domain Name System (DNS). Just as your address book can tell you that your friend Joe Smith lives at 10 High Street, Cambridge, DNS can tell the rider that www.cnn.com "lives" at IP address 157.166.266.25, for example. With the address, the rider is off to that destination.

As with the Pony Express, the trip to the storage location and back is not direct. The rider has to stop at several locations (known as routers or "hops") between the starting point (your browser) and final destination (the Web server) to ask for directions. There can be twenty or more stops for each trip. At each stop, the rider has to ask for directions to the final address. Unfortunately, the staff at the stop does not actually know how to get to the final destination. Rather, they use a tool called the Border Gateway Protocol (BGP), which tells them only the next stop on the journey. Eventually, the rider makes it to the storage facility, asks for the Web file, retrieves it, then heads back to your browser using the same method used to get there—traversing the various "hops" and routes along the way. The rider may stop at the same locations on the return trip or take a completely different route.

Once the rider returns, your browser opens the file and notices that there are a bunch of related objects needed to view the complete Web page—pictures, videos, ads, etc. In this case, the rider must be dispatched again to the same storage facility, this time to retrieve all the component parts. Each page can have twenty to thirty related objects—only one of which the rider can collect at a time—and the storage facility can be thousands of miles away. All of this makes the process of getting a complete Web page time-consuming and cumbersome. It is worth noting that, while the initial Web page file is usually small, the related objects can be big and unwieldy (videos, for example), making them difficult to transport.

While this whole process sounds quite tedious, there is one thing that makes it relatively quick—light or, more accurately, the speed of light. Most of the stops on the rider's journey are connected by fiber optic cables, which allow the rider to travel the roads between stops at the speed of light—186,000 miles per second. That's fast enough to circle the globe seven times in one second. So, while the stops are many and the distance great, the speed is fast enough to mask the challenges, at least most of the time.

Still today, the potential problems with this system include the following:

1. Lots of riders may be asking the DNS server for addresses, leading to delays.

2. The stops might be closed, forcing the rider to backtrack and find an alternate route.

3. There might be a lot of riders on the roads between stops, leading to congestion and delays.

4. There might be a lot of riders at the stops asking for directions leading to further delays.

5. The storage facility itself might be closed.

6. There might be lots of riders at the storage facility asking for files, leading to more delays.

There are a few ways to mitigate these potential problems, and one of the most popular is called "caching." The idea behind caching is straightforward: it's a method that moves Web content closer to the user requesting it. Rather than forcing the rider to travel across many hops, a copy of the requested files are kept at a storage location closer to the browser known as a cache server. This way the rider only has to travel two or three hops to the cache server to get the file, rather than the twenty hops on the route to the original file storage facility. Not only does this make for a shorter trip; it also decreases the likelihood of running into problems during the longer journey. While this sounds quite simple in theory, in practice caches can be hard to manage.

For these reasons and more, the Internet was experiencing intense growing pains in the 1990s. By late 1995, networking pioneer Robert "Bob" Metcalfe of MIT's Project MAC sounded the alarm in a string of speeches, columns, and interviews. "The Internet has outgrown its design and needs to be fixed," he argued. "There are going to be more outages, and they're going to get worse." In October, the Associated Press ran a story with the headline "Is the Internet Poised to Collapse?" in which journalist Elizabeth Weise wrote: "The Internet is broken. The evidence is everywhere. Outages drop millions offline for hours, sometimes days. The number of users has been doubling every year since 1988, and traffic on some long-distance routes doubles every four months. World Wide Web pages take forever to load because data pipes are clogged."[5] It was a pressing problem, and one that was also on the mind of British physicist and computer scientist Tim Berners-Lee, known as the inventor of the World Wide Web.

Berners-Lee moved to Cambridge in 1994 to found the W3C, an international body charged with governing the standards for the Internet. He came from CERN, the European Laboratory for Particle Physics, where he wrote the software that would eventually open the Web browser and provide its underlying protocol. Specifically, he created the hypertext markup language, or HTML, and the hypertext transfer protocol, the http:// that precedes the zillions of Web addresses (i.e., URLs) that are now as ubiquitous as ZIP codes. HTML, a coding language, provided a framework for enabling users to access electronic documents in a standard way. It also meant links could be built into documents themselves so that they could be connected together, rather than existing as separate and distinct pieces of data.

One day, Berners-Lee, whose W3C office shared a floor with MIT's theory group, walked down the hall to talk with Leighton about what he called the "hot spot" problem. The Web was not running smoothly, with bottlenecks contributing to a challenge Berners-Lee termed the "World Wide Wait." Leighton had a crew of graduate students working on a better way to manage and distribute content over the Web, and Berners-Lee asked if they could come up with a way, mathematically, to scale the Internet. Leighton wasn't sure his group could find a solution, but he said they would try. "In many ways Tim presented an ideal problem for me and my group to work on," Leighton said. "We didn't understand the Internet that well, but we knew a lot about the way information flowed and the math behind it, and we wanted to find an answer."

Finding one, Leighton knew, was not going to be easy. In the race to end the World Wide Wait, engineers and computer scientists had developed a patchwork of quick fixes, but a lasting solution eluded them at every turn. The problem was simple to state, but the answer was nearly impossible to put a finger on. It wasn't even clear in which direction to look. The fix lay somewhere in the nexus of the network of networks—the ill defined, tangled, seemingly infinite wilderness of the Internet. In the search for an answer, no one was betting on the theory group. But infinity doesn't scare theoretical mathematicians. And it certainly didn't scare Danny Lewin.

CHAPTER 2

Ascent to Israel

"Who dares wins."

—MOTTO OF SAYERET MATKAL,
otherwise known as "the Unit"

From a young age, Danny Lewin brandished what his parents called "extraordinary vigor," building impenetrable fortresses, constructing homemade computers, and climbing the foothills surrounding his early home in Englewood, Colorado. The Lewin family enjoyed an enviable, middle-class existence in the suburb of Denver, where they settled just before Danny, their eldest son, was born on May 14, 1970. Both Charles and Peggy, his parents, worked in medicine, Charles as a child and adolescent psychiatrist with a busy private practice and Peggy as a pediatrician for the Denver hospital health program. They owned a spacious home—a contemporary-style house they designed—in the quiet neighborhood of Greenwood Village, filled with young families. They attended Temple Sinai, a Reform Jewish synagogue where Danny celebrated his bar mitzvah.

As an eighth grade student at Cherry Creek Middle School, Danny was a popular kid: he skied, flirted with girls, and excelled in both academics and athletics. The three Lewin boys—Danny, Jonathan, and Michael—were all extraordinarily gifted. But of the brothers, Danny had seemingly limitless talents of such broad scope they were often a study in contradiction. With thick, beefy hands like bear paws, he could effortlessly grip a barbell to bench-press yet also play a delicate instrument like the violin masterfully. He could bark orders with the intensity of a drill sergeant yet also sing so beautifully he landed starring roles in the musicals staged at his synagogue, often committing all his lines to heart the night before the performance. The only thing he couldn't do well, according to his parents, was play soccer, which frustrated him to no end.

Peggy and Charles Lewin created a household that thrived on intellectual pursuits. Charles taught the boys music, literature, art, and science. For the Lewins, learning was a game—and Charles was the ringleader. He could turn almost anything, even routine family chores and meals, into an educational experience. Michael and Jonathan remember their initial dismay when their father pasted over the cartoons on the backs of their cereal boxes with math puzzles and snippets from *Scientific American* magazine. His nighttime stories became an event worth going to bed for; he would spin some fabulous tale into a problem-solving game, delighting and challenging his sons. "We enjoyed it," said Michael Lewin. "My father always pushed us to excel; he wanted us to be interested in real things and not just sit around and listen to the television."

Charles Lewin also introduced his sons to technology, inspiring in all of them an early interest in computers. Before the advent of the personal computer (PC) in the early 1970s, Charles purchased a kit to assemble a computer himself. The Altair didn't have a keyboard or a video display, but, for early enthusiasts like Charles, the ability to input data into the machine was thrilling. In 1979, he brought home an Apple II, one of the first successful PCs designed by Apple co-founder Steve Wozniak. The Lewins became the only family in their neighborhood to own one, and the three boys—then ages five, seven and nine—spent countless hours teaching themselves how to program it.

Over the years, however, Charles Lewin had begun to feel increasingly dissatisfied with his comfortable Colorado life. It wasn't unhappiness he suffered, but a nagging sense of restlessness. "I felt there had to be more to life," explained Charles. A prolific poet (who later self-published several collections of his work under the pen name Yaakov Ben David), Charles was a serious, introspective man who loathed the trappings of material wealth. In search of a greater purpose in life, he turned to Zionism, the international movement for the return of the Jewish people to their homeland. Gradually, Charles's identification with Zionism intensified, and he began to seriously consider a move to Israel. The longer he remained in Colorado, the more he felt his Jewish identity being threatened by the shadowy specter of assimilation.

The best thing for himself and his family, he believed, was for them to "make *aliyah*," or immigrate to Israel. Translated literally from Hebrew, *aliyah* means "ascent"—a term used to describe the repatriation of the Jews to Israel. Returning to the their homeland has long been an aspiration for Jews and a core belief of Zionism. It was rare for Americans to make *aliyah*, and those who did were usually motivated by deep ideological yearnings. In 1984, when Charles began planning his family's departure from Colorado, successfully making *aliyah* with a family of older children was almost unheard of. That year, approximately 2,827 American families made *aliyah*, and, of those, it's estimated only a fraction remained permanently in Israel—the majority returning to America frustrated by the challenges of relocating and missing the ease of life back home.

To ease the shock of his sudden decision to move, Charles presented the plan as a temporary, yearlong trial. His family knew better. While Peggy reluctantly agreed to the move, the three Lewin boys, Danny, Jonathan, and Michael—then ages fourteen, twelve, and ten, respectively—did *not* want to leave the U.S. And they let their parents know it. If anything could have pulled apart the close-knit family in the move, it was the powerful force of teenage fury. When it came time to leave, Danny cried, shouted, and complained, but Charles was not to be dissuaded. "I thought that, finally, we were doing something that we didn't quite fully understand where it would lead us or what it could be," Charles explained. "But it had a sense of purposefulness and fulfillment for our lives as Jews."

On July 24, 1984, the Lewins arrived in Haifa, Israel, and began the difficult process of assimilation. They spoke no Hebrew and had no jobs and no real friends or family to help ease their transition. And the Israel that greeted Danny and his family when they arrived that summer was not exactly welcoming. Like most new immigrants, the Lewins first stop was a *merkaz klita*, a state-run absorption program that provides housing, support, and *ulpan* (Hebrew school). The Lewins chose to live at an absorption center in the mountainous city of Mevaseret Zion on the outskirts of Jerusalem. Those first months put a strain on the entire family, one so clear to the center's other residents that they voted the Lewins the "least likely to stay." But they did stay, and after three months at the center, Peggy and Charles decided it was time to find a home of their own. They settled into a rented apartment in the French Hill section of Jerusalem, a diverse neighborhood densely populated with immigrants from all over the world. The Apple II, which withstood the long journey from Colorado, came with them.

For new immigrants to Israel, even with government assistance, opening a bank account was fraught with obstacles. Until the late 1980s, obtaining a telephone from Bezeq, the state-owned company that had a monopoly on the country's telecommunications, often took more than a year and required *protekzia* (contacts) to sidestep a waiting list of hundreds of thousands.[1] If you were lucky enough to have a television set, it had only one grainy channel, the state-sponsored Channel One. In addition to logistical challenges, the Lewins also faced the daily possibility of violence. Although the start of the First Intifada was still three years away, terrorism was an everyday part of life. In the early 1980s, Jerusalem alone saw dozens of bombings attributed to Palestinian guerrilla groups. In 1984, the city police reported the explosion of forty-one devices—in shopping bags, on sidewalks, even in an aluminum can—which killed seven and wounded fifty-eight.[2]

To restart their careers, Charles and Peggy had to remain in Hebrew classes for six months, enough time to learn the spoken and written proficiency they needed to work. After this, they began three-month rotations at a hospital, jobs that paid almost nothing but were required by the state to practice specialized medicine. In early 1985, Charles started working at a city clinic in Jerusalem, supervising psychologists and psychiatric residents. Peggy found two part-time jobs, one as a pediatrician at a French Hill practice owned by a classmate from her residency program in New York, the other in general pediatrics at a city clinic in Mea She'arim, an ultra-orthodox neighborhood in Jerusalem. To treat her Hasidic patients, Peggy had to work with a Yiddish translator. Resuming work was even more challenging for Charles. In anticipation of the move, he took Hebrew classes in Colorado, but even after studying it another six months in Jerusalem, he found it almost impossible to conduct therapy sessions in Hebrew. Because of this, he joined a private practice where he began to build a roster of English-speaking adult and child patients.

A year passed, and by this time it was clear the move to Israel from Denver was not a temporary one for the Lewins. "Charles said he would go back to America [if I asked him to], but that it would be like living death," said Peggy. "I was married to him, and a living death was not an option, so we stayed."

With his broken Hebrew and a heavy American accent, Danny Lewin began his sophomore year at Ort, a science and technology high school on the campus of Hebrew University. The transition from his easy, all-American adolescence to an Israeli high school with few English speakers was a troubled one. While he eventually made friends at Ort and earned high marks in all his classes, Lewin didn't quickly fit in with his classmates, tough *sabras* (native-born Israelis) who were already preparing, mentally and physically, for compulsory military service after graduation. In many ways, Lewin had lost his adolescence

In the spring of 1985, while waiting for his school bus, Lewin met a twenty-one-year-old neighbor named Brad Rephen. Born in Brooklyn, New York, Rephen had moved to Israel with his younger brother to study at Hebrew University. He planned a return to New York—until the day his parents called him from Ben Gurion airport to tell him that they had decided to make *aliyah*. Rephen, who spoke both English and Hebrew fluently and had a group of international friends, was quick to connect with Lewin. Rephen was pursuing a degree in political science at the university, but spent most of his time training for service in the Israeli army at a local hot spot: Samson's Gym. An American-style fitness center, the recently opened gym was already generating buzz in Jerusalem, attracting an imposing mix of buff American and Israeli men. Rephen told Lewin about the gym and invited him to come by. At the time, he didn't think the baby-faced teenager would have the *chutzpah* (courage) to show up at the gym on his own. Days later, he spotted Lewin in line at Samson's, signing up for a membership. Although he had not a trace of tough guy in his face, Lewin was pure strength from head to toe. Of average weight and height, he was muscular and agile, the kind of guy who left a bruise when he playfully slugged someone in the shoulder.

Still stinging from the involuntary move, Lewin was struggling to fit in at school. Among *olim hadashim* (new immigrants) to Israel, there's an unspoken contest to see who is the first to learn Hebrew and adopt Israeli mannerisms. Lewin had accomplished neither, so he made Samson's his home away from home as an outlet for his frustration. His new friends remember him training so hard that his physical strength multiplied. He worked out until he was blue in the face and his muscles failed, all while sweating and sputtering commands to push himself. "He resented the fact that his parents had taken him out of his environment," Rephen said. "But he wasn't angry at them, he was angry at his situation. He needed to find himself again, and he did it at Samson's." Rephen still remembers Lewin's efforts to fit in with the confident, sometimes brash Samson's crew, which included Lewin sharing charming, but likely embellished, tales of his romantic conquests back in Colorado.

Although he didn't always attend school, Lewin aced it, sailing through his classes at Ort without too much effort. Friends say he often skipped classes to spend time at Samson's, but if he did, Peggy and Charles Lewin were never aware of it. In fact, Peggy Lewin says she remembered Danny working well into the night on projects for physics and science, masterful constructions that earned him top marks. Not surprisingly, Lewin didn't advertise his intellectual prowess at Samson's, where you rose to the status of cool by brute force, not brains. But he was always learning, and friends recall moments when they realized Lewin was a force to be reckoned with outside the gym.

"I had Shabbat dinner with his family a few times, and that's when it struck me that they were all really unique," noted Ronen Sarig, who also met Lewin at the gym. "I think Danny was often trying to dumb himself down to fit in, but when I met his family, I realized his parents were really trying to guide their kids to something big and important in life, and that Danny and his brothers were really smart."

But Charles and Peggy Lewin were also working hard, pushing to get their careers in a new country off the ground. And while Danny's anger at his parents diminished over time, he didn't want to be at home much. In his own way, he emancipated himself from his family and their French Hill apartment, spending all his spare time outside of school at Samson's.

By the time he was sixteen, Lewin could bench press more than 300 pounds, a noteworthy weight for someone of his age and build, making him somewhat of a spectacle at Samson's. In the summer of 1986, a twenty-two-year-old college student from Beverly Hills named Marco Greenberg arrived at Samson's to sign up for a membership.

While waiting in line, another American student named Roger Abramson grabbed Greenberg by the arm and said, "Come here, you've go to see this kid."

Despite a six-year age difference, Greenberg and Lewin became fast friends. The two had many things in common: childhood years in Colorado, a love for American culture and a keen intellect, to name a few. To Lewin, Greenberg was no doubt a reminder of home. But he was also evidence of the fact that Israel, for many, was an appealing place to live. Greenberg had come to Israel voluntarily to study for a summer at Hebrew University before his last semester at University of California, Los Angeles. Raised in Colorado and southern Los Angeles, Greenberg was tall and good-looking, and practically exuded California cool. Pursuing a double major in history and political science, he, like Lewin, had a passion for news and politics. Greenberg was struck by how much wiser, and more mature, Lewin seemed than his sixteen years. He could see Lewin's struggle as he continued to straddle two worlds, but he also saw in him the makings of an extraordinary friend. "He had this amazing energy and warmth," Greenberg recalled. "And an incredible ability to make people feel good about themselves."

Lewin's good cheer could have been one of the reasons he didn't assimilate quickly. Israelis are notorious skeptics, priding themselves on a serious, "no bullshit" attitude that often eschews small talk and superficial expressions of enthusiasm in favor of communicating with efficiency and candor. Lewin actually liked the Israeli way, though, often mocking American waitresses, for example, for their forced joviality. But in many ways, Lewin embodied American optimism. He was a hugger, a high-fiver, and a constant smiler. Even his writing style could not contain his natural gusto; he often ended sentences with multiple exclamation points, a stylistic choice he never surrendered, even years later when drafting business-related e-mails.

Together, Greenberg and Lewin spent the summer of 1986, and the first half of 1997 (when Greenberg returned to Israel after college graduation) exploring Israel in between workouts at the gym—hitting the beaches of Tel Aviv, courting exotic Mediterranean girls, and taking day trips into the desert or mountains. "It was like a *shouk* (marketplace), literally and figuratively," Greenberg said. "There we were, two American guys strolling the streets, hopping in taxis, traveling, meeting girls." Still, it wasn't yet clear to Lewin's friends, or even his family, that he would one day be capable of deeply understanding the high-level math and computer science expected at MIT. "He was wickedly funny, and outside his tough, macho image, he was such a nice character," testified Ronen Sarig. "But if you asked me at the time if I thought he was a genius, I would have said no." In part, this was because Lewin—like almost all Israeli teenagers—wasn't talking about college as his next step. He had his eyes on the army.

Lewin's interest in the army began at Samson's, where he often lifted weights alongside commandos just back from missions with stunning tales of jumping out of airplanes, trudging miles in the desert, and surviving firefights with terrorists. The Samson's crew not only talked terrorism, they lived it. Rephen still recalls the frequent bomb scares on Ben Yehuda Street; in fact, he once heard the explosion of a yellow duffel bag he'd seen at the bus stop where he and Lewin often met.

At age eighteen, all Israelis begin a minimum of two years of army service. Even though military service wasn't required for a non-native, Lewin hadn't spent two years building the physical strength of a warrior and fighting to integrate into Israeli life just to leave without joining up, too. With his classmates and friends facing military training, Lewin didn't hesitate. School, he told friends, could wait. Lewin dropped his training at the gym down to just two days a week to shed some of his muscle mass in preparation for the army.

To increase his stamina, he also began running. He often ran at night, and Rephen still remembered the sight of Lewin jogging the streets of Jerusalem at dusk for hours at a time. If he was going to be in the army, Lewin told friends, he was going to be in one of the best fighting units.

Recruitment into a "good fighting unit" is an almost universal goal among combatants who want to be in the IDF's voluntary units, and Lewin had his sights on the most elite of them: Sayeret Matkal. Even for Lewin, with his exceptional intelligence and physical prowess, it was an audacious goal. The skills and operations of Sayeret Matkal warriors are the stuff of legend in Israel, and joining its ranks is a rarity—even for the best soldiers. The Unit's commandos were handpicked—often from the sons, nephews or cousins of former Matkalists—until the 1980s, when the IDF opened its recruitment camps to volunteers.[3]

By the 1990s the selection process for Sayeret Matkal had expanded significantly, but for soldiers who were not Israeli-born, recruitment to Sayeret Matkal was almost unheard of. Still, Lewin made the first of many decisions in his short life to defy the odds.

The Israeli army has a reputation for military strikes on some of the world's most dangerous terrorist organizations. If there's one unit of the IDF responsible for these daring exploits, it's Sayeret Matkal, also known as the General Staff Reconnaissance Unit, the Chief of Staff's Boys, or simply "the Unit."

The Unit was formed in 1957 to carry out top-secret intelligence gathering missions in enemy territory without attracting public attention. One of its most decorated soldiers, Ehud Barak, took the reins two years later. Barak is credited with shaping Sayeret Matkal into one of the world's most deadly and effective counterterrorism forces. Although Sayeret Matkal is often compared to America's Navy Seals and Britain's Special Air Service (SAS), military experts put the Unit in a class of its own because of its near mythical status.[4]

In *The Elite*, author Samuel M. Katz defines the type of warrior the early leaders of Sayeret Matkal recruited, a tradition that still holds true today: "The commanders of the unit were not looking for cold-blooded killers, nor did they seek robots who would follow orders blindly. They sought innovative men who could, like spies, work alone behind enemy lines, and, like guerrillas, improvise with skill, determination, and well-directed firepower when operating in hostile surroundings."[5] The soldiers in the brigade must also possess above average intelligence and technological savvy, so they are capable of handling and operating the IDF's most prized technological equipment.

Until the 1990s, Sayeret Matkal was so important to Israel's security that the IDF would not officially acknowledge its existence. Those who knew anything about its inner workings were sworn to a code of silence, and its soldiers are still forbidden to wear its insignia in public. But like many big secrets, some of the most spectacular, action movie-like missions of Sayeret Matkal have come to light eventually, most of them leaked initially by the foreign media. The unit is best known for its 1976 raid on an airport in Uganda's capital of Entebbe, when commandos rescued 103 hostages from a gang of Arab terrorists. Prime Minister Benjamin Netanyahu's brother, Yonatan, commanded the mission and was killed carrying it out. Today, the IDF officially acknowledges Sayeret Matkal as "the best combat unit," but the details of its day-to-day operations remain classified; many are intelligence-gathering missions carried out behind enemy lines.

The IDF's recruitment process is intense, and begins sometime during the final two years of high school for all Israeli citizens with an initial, daylong screening process. From the tens of thousands who try out, the IDF selects a few thousand recruits who are eligible to participate in a one-day test camp called *gibushon*. Those who pass proceed to a five-day test camp, called *gibbush*, held months later. This camp is so grueling that doctors and psychologists constantly monitor the recruits throughout the process, which involves long stretches without sleep and repetitive, exhausting physical and mental tasks. The purpose of the *gibbush* is to weed out those who lack the mental toughness to withstand the pressures and potential perils of highly secretive missions. From this test, anywhere from 20–40 men are selected for Sayeret Matkal. Of those chosen, only one is promoted to the rank of officer.

Members of Sayeret Matkal must endure almost two years of intense physical and mental training before they fully qualify to be Matkal commandos, which includes advanced navigation, weapons training and a sniper's course.[6]

The Beret March, named for the beret that soldiers earn if they complete the training, is a long, arduous trek through remote terrain between Tel Aviv and Jerusalem. All IDF soldiers complete a march to enter their respective army units, each march with varying distances depending on the unit. The regular infantry units—Nahal, Givati, and Golani—march about 45 kilometers. Special units—Oketz and Tzanhanim—march approximately 65 kilometers. And the most elite units, including Sayeret Matkal, march about 125 kilometers (75 miles). The march is one of the most important accomplishments, both physically and psychologically, for soldiers in the Special Forces.[7]

To complete his own Beret March in 1988, Lewin walked through remote swathes of the country for about twenty-five hours alongside his platoon of about twenty-five. He walked through the night, with only the stars to guide him in territory so dark it was hard to see his own hand in front of his face. He climbed hills and scaled craggy cliffs under the weight of sixty pounds of gear on his back. Several hours into the march, all of the soldiers, including Danny, felt their feet burning from erupting blisters. Twenty hours in some of them began slipping in and out of stages of delirium, walking as if they were asleep and occasionally veering out of the formation. By the time they reached the end of the march, the soldiers were too exhausted to enjoy the fraternity-like reception given by elder commanders at the finish line. That day, or sometime that week, IDF commanders awarded Lewin with the coveted red beret—a symbol of membership in the Unit—and he was welcomed into Sayeret Matkal.

Even after only a year of service, some of Lewin's exploits—though almost all of them remain secret—had become legendary to soldiers who served with him. In the most select unit of what is arguably one of the toughest armies in the world, Lewin pushed himself beyond what was expected.

Lior Netzer, a friend who served with Lewin in Sayeret Matkal and later worked with him, remembered his surprise when he passed Lewin during a training session involving a ten-mile, hilly walk weighted down with full gear of about 50 pounds. Lewin was known as a strong walker in these types of exercises, rarely showing any visible signs of fatigue. On this particular walk, although he completed it on time, Lewin seemed to be struggling, often crouching down to rest and catch his breath. When asked to explain, Lewin confessed that he had voluntarily doubled his load of gear to prove to himself that he could still finish.

In 1991, three years after earning his spot in the unit, Lewin was promoted to the rank of officer. His unit trained all week when they were not called on missions, departing on Sunday nights and returning on Fridays for Shabbat with their families. Lewin's younger brothers—who both went on to serve in the IDF—remembered him arriving home covered in dust, sand, and scratches, deeply suntanned from long days of training in the desert, and exhausted from a week of only a few hours of sleep. They also recalled that over time, Danny's army service ignited in him fervent political ideals; he became what Jonathan Lewin called a "super Zionist," committed to defending Israel and wiping out terrorism. Prone to hyperbole, Danny was unafraid to express his views, often commanding the dinner table during Shabbat meals with exaggerated rants about destroying Israel's enemies. "As a soldier he believed that it was his job to risk his life to fight against people who were trying to do evil in the world," Jonathan said. "Danny had a very clear view that the way to address terrorism was not to sit idly by and let innocent people be killed, but to actively go out and cut the head off the stick."

Because of the Unit's code of silence, the details of Lewin's missions in Sayeret Matkal are not known. In interviews, veterans of the Unit are reluctant to share their names, even when describing general training. What has been leaked only in recent years is that, during the period in which Lewin served (1988–1991), Sayeret Matkal is believed to have carried out two exceptional missions—the 1998 assassination of Abu Jihad, Yasir Arafat's military commander, and the July 1989 kidnapping of Sheikh Obeid, Hezbollah's commander in Southern Lebanon.

It's also known that the Unit is Israel's secret weapon when combating terrorism. In a December 2001 article in *Vanity Fair*, journalist Rich Cohen wrote: "When facing terrorism, especially in the wake of awful events, there is a tendency to despair, to see in the battle a problem without a solution. The functioning of the Unit is therefore more than merely a practical solution; it is a philosophical response. The simple act of resistance is in itself a key victory over terrorism."[8]

In addition to almost unmatched counterterrorism skills, those who serve in the Unit are automatically welcomed into an influential old-boys' club that opens doors in the worlds of politics, business and other areas of Israeli society. In Israel, where one's academic past is often less important than military past, the mention of service in Sayeret Matkal can act as a golden ticket to top jobs and political positions.

Of the time he spent with Lewin in the unit, Lior Netzer said, "It is a place where you experience things that I can tell you I have not experienced ever since. You never get to push yourself to those limits. I can't think [of] anything you can do at that age where you have that much responsibility."

When Lewin wasn't on duty and returned home to Jerusalem, he turned to another passion typical of young men his age: women. He had no trouble finding dates. Dressed in his crisply pressed military uniform, he was often the object of attraction among the young ladies at local bars or clubs. In late 1990, at the apartment of a friend in Jerusalem, Lewin met a pretty, sweet twenty-one-year-old Belgian with green eyes and soft brown curls named Anne Pardes. Like Lewin, Anne had moved to Israel as a teenager with her family, also inspired by a Zionist wave. Their courtship, like all things in Lewin's life, was impassioned and intense. Lewin almost instantly decided he wanted to spend the rest of his life with Anne, and he began tirelessly wooing her with romantic outings and hand-written poems and notes. Just six months after taking Anne out for the first time for a night of dancing, Lewin borrowed his parent's car, an old white station wagon, and drove Anne to one of his favorite spots outside Jerusalem. There, on a cliff overlooking a vast expanse of desert, he surprised Anne by asking her to marry him. Anne didn't hesitate, and the two became engaged. Although Lewin was still spending weeks away from home for army training and missions, he and Anne moved into an apartment together and made plans to wed later that year.

His service duties intensified in January 1991 with the start of the Gulf War. With U.S. troops positioned at the border of Saudi

Arabia, Iraqi President Saddam Hussein declared that if the U.S. launched an attack, Iraq would respond with a missile strike against Israel. Late in the night on January 18, Iraqi forces fired forty-two SCUD-B missiles into Tel Aviv and Haifa, killing two and severely damaging Ramat Gan, a suburb of Tel Aviv. As missiles from Iraq continued to rain down over the course of several weeks, Israeli citizens carried out the routine they had practiced many times over: when the air raid sirens began to wail, they took their gas masks and retreated to the basements of their buildings and homes. At the Lewins' invitation, Anne stayed with Peggy and Charles while Danny was away, and together they spent weeks on high alert—donning gas masks and hiding in the basement when the air raid sirens wailed.

Based somewhere in the center of Israel, Lewin wrote to Marco Greenberg during the height of the attacks. With the looming threat of war in the region, Lewin expressed doubts about remaining in the military:

> As you can probably imagine, the general atmosphere here is quite tense. But surprisingly, the army seems to be much more relaxed than the civilian population. The streets of Tel Aviv after five o'clock are about as populated as the deserts of Saudi Arabia, and the nightlife has come to an unanticipated halt. The whole city sits peevishly waiting for the wail of the air raid siren [and] listening to the perpetual newscasts. In comparison, the army is unaffected by the missile attacks. Training continues as usual, and when there is a siren, people calmly file into the sealed rooms, and wait. . . . I personally am a little more disturbed, because my base is in the center of the country. The BOOMs [can] be heard clearly here, and in one case, the windows even broke in some of the buildings.
>
> I try to get home as often as possible to see Anne. She deals with the situation quite well considering the conditions under which

we must carry on our relationship. After we are married (August 20th, to remind you), I should be home more. I am also thinking about requesting a leave from the army in order to go to school. Whether or not I do really depends on what the conclusion of the present situation brings about.

It's possible that Lewin believed his situation would be upended at any time. The world was waiting for Israel to retaliate, and rumors circulated in the press and public discourse that the IDF might dispatch Sayeret Matkal to Baghdad to carry out an Entebbe-like mission.[9] The details of a supposed plan, later reported in *Newsweek*, suggested that the IDF considered sending Sayeret Matkal commandos and agents from Mossad (Israeli intelligence) to infiltrate the Iraqi capital under cover of darkness and execute a number of key individual targets.[10] But Israel didn't act—at all. American military leaders cautioned against an attack, and sent in U.S. forces to commence Operation Desert Storm.

On August 20, 1991, Danny, twenty-one, and Anne, twenty-three, were married in a small ceremony in Jerusalem. It was clear to Lewin's friends that Anne—mild-mannered, smart, and strong-willed—had a grounding effect on him. Greenberg remembered meeting Anne. "She was extremely sophisticated, sensitive, and thoughtful," he observed. "I did think they were [too] young to get married, but I also knew Danny was serious about everything in his life, and for him, it was the right choice. It was the only choice."

Marrying young is also common among native-born, male Israelis whose military experience lends them a heightened sensitivity to the passage of time. In their book *Start-Up Nation*, Dan Senor and Saul Singer explain: "Since their country's founding, Israelis have [been] keenly aware that the future—both near and distant—is always in question. Every moment has strategic importance."[11]

Months later, Lewin requested leave from the IDF to attend the Technion (Israeli Institute of Technology). He and Anne were expecting their first son, Eitan, and Anne was eager to relocate to the quiet, scenic city of Haifa to begin their life together. But even Haifa couldn't slow Lewin down. About two years into his studies at the Technion, Lewin came across a textbook at the library on the topic of parallel algorithms. He was so moved by its depth and beauty that he brought it home, pulling it out of his backpack and telling Anne that he'd never seen such incredible research. Lewin became fixated on the book and its author, MIT Professor Tom Leighton, inspired solely on what he'd learned from the pages of the massive tome. He told Anne that he was determined to meet Leighton. At the time, Lewin's pursuit of the MIT professor must have sounded a bit outlandish to family or friends. For Lewin, however, it was nothing but sincere. He applied to and was accepted to MIT, and after less than four years in Haifa, the young family was packing for Cambridge—Anne pregnant with their second son, Itamar.

CHAPTER 3

Publish or Perish

"I'll tell you once,
and I'll tell you again.
There's always a prime
between n and 2n."

—PAUL ERDOS,
Topics in the Theory of Numbers

The most challenging problems in mathematics have never frustrated Professor Tom Leighton. He can reel off the names of mathematical mysteries—P vs. NP, the Riemann Hypothesis, and infinity—that have confounded great scientists for centuries. To him, they are exciting and intellectually invigorating—puzzles waiting to be solved in some eureka moment that gives rise to boundless possibility.

Born October 28, 1956, Leighton grew up in Arlington, Virginia, a suburb of Washington, D.C. From an early age, math spoke to him, and he understood it so well that even he suspects it was partly hereditary. Leighton can't trace his gift to any precise origin, but thinks it may have come from his grandmother, a natural mathematician who taught him his multiplication tables as a child. Leighton also credits his parents, both smart and studious. His mother, Helen, was a librarian. And his father, David, was a nuclear engineer with degrees from both the Naval Academy and MIT. Reporting directly to Admiral Hyman Rickover, David Leighton spent twenty-six years designing and constructing nuclear-powered naval warships. Although he wasn't a mathematician by profession, he loved math and science. With his two sons, Tom and David, he spent time constructing radios and experimenting with chemistry sets.

By the time Tom Leighton, the eldest, was in high school, he was a straight-A student who preferred burying himself in books and wrestling with math problems to parties and football games. During his junior year at Washington–Lee High School in Virginia, he became fixated on one puzzle in particular: Goldbach's Conjecture. For centuries, mathematicians have tried, and failed, to prove the conjecture, which was first proposed by eighteenth-century mathematician Christian Goldbach in 1742. At the heart of the conjecture are prime numbers, or integers, that can't be divided by anything. The conjecture itself, simply put, claims that any even number can be expressed as the sum of two prime numbers. For example:

3 + 5 = 8
3 + 3 = 6
3 + 7 = 10

This goes on and on. There are an infinite number of prime numbers; the proof of this is not hard. But to date, no one has succeeded in proving the theorem by showing that the pattern goes on forever. All of the even numbers up to 400,000,000,000 have been tested, so far, with no exceptions found. But it has never been proven. The combination is seemingly infinite.

At the age of fifteen, Tom Leighton set out to solve the conjecture for his junior year science project. He didn't succeed, but learned a lot of math in the process. He also landed a spot in the National Science Fair. In 1974, Leighton was selected as a finalist in the Westinghouse Science Talent Search (now the Intel Science Talent Search), for which he earned a scholarship to college. As the valedictorian of his class, Leighton had many colleges to choose from. He settled on Princeton University, beginning his freshman year in 1975. Leighton wanted to major in math, but his father, a practical man, steered him toward engineering, which he felt would offer his son much more lucrative career prospects. But Leighton's love for math couldn't be tempered, so he compromised by majoring in both electrical engineering and computer science and by taking courses mostly centered on math.

When Leighton arrived at Princeton, he had no experience with computers and only a cursory knowledge of their history at the university, which dates back to the 1930s and the work of several great, mathematically inclined computer scientists, including Oswald Veblen, John von Neumann, and Alan Turing. Their combined efforts led to the construction of the world's third computer at Princeton's Institute for Advanced Study. With separate units for input and output, the colossal machine was used for everything from weather predictions and evolution studies to the modeling of freeway traffic patterns.[1]

During Leighton's time at Princeton, the Chairman of the university's Electrical Engineering and Computer Science Department edited the results of a six-year research study into one of the most important publications in the field of theoretical computer science. In *What Can Be Automated?* the authors argued that computer science is mainly concerned with fundamental questions in math for two reasons. First, computers and programs are inherently mathematical objects—they manipulate formal symbols, and their input-output can be described by mathematical functions. Second, computer programs are often filled with massive amounts of data, making the number of possible inputs infinite. There is no better way to understand infinite cases, they wrote, than math.[2]

The work at Princeton inspired Leighton's early interest in theoretical computer science, the intersection between math and computing. At the time, very few universities even had departments of computer science, and even fewer offered the study of computer theory. So when Leighton graduated from Princeton, hoping to pursue a higher degree in topics like graph theory and parallel algorithms, his next step was clear. In 1978, he arrived at MIT at the very same time LCS was busy creating ARPANET, the forerunner to the Internet. But Leighton had other interests. "Honestly, I didn't even know what ARPANET was at the time," he said. "I came to MIT for one reason: great theoretical computer science."

In his spare time, Leighton said he and his classmates perpetuated the stereotype of math nerds by staying up all night to play one of the first distributed videogames, Spacewar.[3] Leighton learned to code programs, but never mastered the skill or joined the hackers who spent hours glued to computer screens. Instead, he remained squarely focused on an emerging field in theory: parallel distributed algorithms.

By this time, it seemed Leighton's father had been correct— math, even in computer science, was not a ticket to fortune or fame. But Leighton didn't care. "MIT was the most wonderful place to be and to research," he said.

Two decades later in the late 1990s, Leighton was more than comfortably entrenched at MIT, where he'd risen to the head of the theory group at LCS, then the algorithms group. In these positions, Leighton worked closely with young scientists from all corners of the globe, and they were nothing but the best. In 1996, LCS accepted just one hundred students out of a pool of more than two thousand applicants. Of those, only five joined Leighton's theory group, including Lewin himself. Even by the exacting standards of MIT, it was an exceptional year.

In addition to Lewin, the theory group's cast of characters included the following: Yevgeniy Dodis of Moldova, who immigrated to America with his parents in the 1970s to attend college at New York University (back in Moldova, Dodis was a celebrity, the three-time winner of the tiny country's high school math championship); Eric Lehman, a whiz kid from North Dakota who studied computer science in college at MIT; Salil Vadhan, a Harvard graduate with a passion for complexity theory; and Amit Sahai, a Berkeley computer genius and winner of the Association for Computing Machinery's World Programming Championship. They were joined the following year by Ukrainian cryptographer Anna Lysyanskaya, one of just two female students at LCS, and Venkat Gurwasami from India, whom everyone agreed was the smartest of them all.

They were young, serious, and, for the first time in their adult lives, surrounded by people with similar skills and ambition. While some students at LCS felt the tug of the dot-com craze—which was already creating a new generation of millionaires out of university dropouts with dazzling ideas—the theory group members were generally content to stay put. "At that time, the startup rush was in the air," said Amit Sahai, now a tenured professor at UCLA. "But we came to MIT thinking, 'We are the serious math types, we will not get caught up in the gold rush.'"

Central command for the theory group was Building NE43, a homely structure in a cluster of MIT buildings known as Tech Square. Located between Broadway and Main Street, Tech Square was architecturally unremarkable, constructed in the 1960s to resemble a bland government agency and already bearing signs of old age. It featured fraying carpets, hissing radiators, and windowless offices. What the building lacked in character, however, it made up for in soul. As the home of both MIT's LCS and Artificial Intelligence (AI) Lab, the walls of Tech Square seemed to emanate a spirit of imagination and innovation. Although it had been scheduled for demolition by the mid-1990s, Tech Square remained home to the class of 1996. And it was a comfortable one, littered with relics of years past in the form of unfinished papers, whiteboards covered in bursts of brilliance, and piles of coffee-stained textbooks. "Graduate students would rotate through, and you could literally dig around and find debris—notes, half-written papers, whatever—from students many, many years before," recalled Eric Lehman, now an engineer at Google.

The theory group occupied the third floor, where both Tom Leighton and World Wide Web founder Tim Berners-Lee had offices. Be Blackburn, the lab secretary, was affectionately called the "den mother" of LCS. Blackburn was known for offering emotional support to students cracking under pressure and for organizing annual social gatherings. One such gathering was a "corn fest," which Blackburn started because so many of the school's international students had never dined on buttery cobs of corn. When they weren't buried in research, students gathered in the third floor "Theory Lounge" to play timed chess or Scrabble, read the newspaper, or warm up their lunch using the only microwave in the nine-story building. Holiday parties were fun but without frills—fruit, crackers, and overly damp blocks of cheese on toothpicks. Occasionally, someone would introduce a case of beer or box of wine, but the parties almost always ended in a return, en masse, to the lab. Late at night, the windows of LCS would often glow with the deep, fluorescent blue of computing terminals. And in the mornings, the lab was littered with the evidence of all-nighters: cardboard pizza boxes, empty soda cans, and the occasional hooded sweatshirt hanging over a chair.

The atmosphere at LCS was genial, but at times intensely competitive. Like any discipline at a world-class university, there was a push—unspoken but ever present—to publish papers. "There's a lot of subconscious pressure," confirmed Yevgeniy Dodis. "You are surrounded by incredibly smart people, and you are searching for a needle in a haystack—one that will make you famous." And Lewin, said Dodis, possessed a somewhat superhuman drive to find that proverbial needle: "Danny would not even sleep, and he had the drive of a complete madman."

If there was one professor the theory group collectively worked to impress, it was Tom Leighton. To the select few who understood the complexity and beauty of his work, Leighton was a star. In addition to Lewin, a few other students had come to MIT, in part, to work with Leighton. One of them was Amit Sahai. "I remember clearly this period of being awe-struck," Sahai said. "I remember the feeling of 'I have this meeting with Tom, and I better have something clever to say.' We were all pretty amazed by him." Of all those in their small group, Sahai noted, "Danny really worked hard to prove himself to Tom."

Despite the competition, the members of the 1996 theory group formed fast friendships and collaborated on much of their work during that first year. Lewin wasn't the first to publish anything of great importance, a fact that frustrated him. But he still managed to impress his brilliance on his classmates in unexpected ways. Salil Vadhan recalled the time he was working in the lab when Lewin excitedly appeared and announced: "I got it!" Vadhan asked what, and Lewin went on to explain that he'd spent some time thinking about Remco Van der Hofstad, head of the Mathematics Genealogy Project in Stockholm, and his theory of inapproximability. It was late, sometime after 9:00 p.m., yet Lewin insisted that Vadhan follow him to a conference room so he could sketch some ideas out on a whiteboard. Before he knew it, Vadhan realized he'd been sitting there for close to three hours listening to Lewin explain his results with a kind of energy and clarity Vadhan said he'll never forget. "It was a brilliant, extremely lucid presentation for someone who had just read and understood that paper," remarked Vadhan, now a professor at Harvard. "To this day, I can still reproduce the results of Hofstad, thanks to Danny."

As self-professed math geeks, some even socially awkward, the theory students were somewhat awed, and a bit mystified, by Lewin. He was the only student with a family of his own, and he delighted in letting Eitan and Itamar tag along with him to Tech Square, where they'd enliven the musty halls with their tiny voices and laughter. In addition to his experience as a parent, Lewin had a military background, which was almost unheard of in the contemporary ranks of LCS. Occasionally he would thrill his classmates with Hollywood-sounding stories of his time as a soldier or his proposal to Anne on a desert cliff. They didn't know much about Lewin's army service besides the various snippets he shared, but they figured he was likely the first computer scientist at MIT to have fought face-to-face with terrorists. Now and then, he shared some fact that left everyone wide-eyed, like how much C4 you need to blow up a van (start with a lot, then scale back).

It was no surprise, then, that almost as soon as the theory students formed friendships, Lewin became their ringleader. And despite the pressures of the program, they had fun. For them, fun equaled hours spent challenging each other with math puzzles. These intellectual jousting matches inspired Lewin and Eric Lehman to organize a game they called Theory Jeopardy, a weekly competition housed in the third floor lounge of Tech Square. Lewin put himself in charge of rallying his classmates to the games in widely circulated e-mails:

FROM: dlewin@mit.lcs.edu
TO: LCS

Theory Jeopardy is an opportunity for Theory graduate students to sharpen their wits, heap ridicule on one another, and avoid work on Thursday night...

The goal is to solve problems in specified Theory categories while simultaneously inventing new problems to challenge the other players. Your score is raised if you solve a problem or if you falsely claim you can (and are not caught). Your score can drop if you falsely claim that you can solve a problem (and are caught) or if you give a problem which appears to be too hard. Your score can also vary if you violate or exploit an Arbitrary Scoring Rule.

The theory students didn't exactly party, so Theory Jeopardy became their pressure release valve, an opportunity to achieve victory in something concrete at a time when most of them were in the throes of open-ended research projects. "It was about as nerdy as you could get," said Lehman. Another stress reliever, and perhaps the most comical, was the department's softball team. The team leader was Leighton, who loved the opportunity to break free from the barrels of LCS and socialize informally with his students. Lewin took charge of the team's practices and game schedule, and, despite an abysmal record, he rallied everyone to the field with the battle cry of a commanding officer. In his softball e-mails, Lewin goaded his classmates to abandon their studies for the sake of the "lean, green, losing machine."

FROM: dlewin@mit.lcs.edu
TO: LCS listserve

Summer Softball has arrived!

Softball is that competitive team game of seven innings closely resembling baseball but played on a smaller diamond with a ball that is larger and softer than a baseball and that is pitched underhand. Ok, that was from "Webster'," and we probably should redefine [it] as: LCS Softball, A team game during which huge quantities of beer and iced tea are consumed, players regularly don't show up, balls are more often dropped than caught, and balls are pitched so slow that even YOU can hit them!

The first practice will be held TOMORROW on one of the MIT fields (start walking from West to East looking for people discussing permutation routing, batting averages, and compiler technologies).

Lewin appointed Yevgeniy Dodis team captain, despite his protestations. As a native of Moldova, Dodis had never watched a game of softball and had no understanding of the rules. Lewin was so convincing, however, that he reluctantly agreed. The games themselves were a spectacle. "We were horrible," recalled Lehman. "Someone would hit a ball, and we'd all run the wrong way trying to catch it. Eventually, it would just bounce on the ground."

The intellectual energy of MIT excited both Danny and Anne; their neighbors were studying to be molecular biologists, biomedical engineers, architects, and so on. In a neighborhood with students from all over the world, the married couple often spent long evenings engaged in heated political or academic debates by the playground in the courtyard of their student housing.

The family's weekends were never spent lounging around the apartment or watching television. Instead, after a long, often grueling week of school, Lewin would greet the boys and Anne first thing Saturday morning with a plan: the zoo, a national park, a campout, or a museum. They took day trips to Newport, Rhode Island, sailed on the Charles River in Massachusetts, and skied in Vermont. When the boys complained of nothing to do, Lewin often replied: "Life is too short to be bored. Only boring people are bored." As if to prove himself, he then typically disappeared into the kitchen, rummaged the cupboards and returned with a haphazard collection of items. As the boys sat captivated, he feverishly whipped up a warrior costume, fashioning a sword out of a spoon wrapped in foil and armor out of bowls and baking sheets.

Fatherhood was something Lewin approached with his characteristic, unbridled enthusiasm. In many ways, Lewin was childlike; he had a sophomoric sense of humor, unrestrained energy, and had an easier time playing with his kids than making small talk at cocktail parties. Although Lewin was a strict disciplinarian, Eitan and Itamar were smitten with him. Lewin always made time for them, skipping out of class in the middle of the day to surprise them at the playground. He built forts, wrestled, and instigated pillow fights with them. Greenberg remembered seeing Lewin changing diapers with a smile on his face, using his large hands to fasten the tiny tabs with military-like precision.

In an interview for a documentary tribute to Danny, Anne recalled the thrill the boys got out of Lewin's "word games." Every week he would comb the dictionary for the quirkiest, strangest-sounding word he could find, write its definition on an index card, and pin it to the fridge "Obstreperous" became one of his favorite words, an ironic choice considering it is used to describe someone who is stubborn, resistant to control, and noisy. Tongue-in-cheek, Lewin used it to describe others, not himself, namely anyone who got in his way. Later, he transformed it into a catch phrase among his co-workers when referring to competitors or naysayers.

That first year in Cambridge wasn't easy for Danny and Anne. They were both in graduate school; Anne was accepted to Boston College, where she decided to pursue a Master's in French Literature. They were both working as Teaching Assistants, and needed help with care for Eitan and Itamar. Fortunately, they found an at-home daycare run by a family from India—Preetish and Shirin Nijhawan. Preetish was a graduate student at MIT's Sloan School of Business, and to make ends meet, Shirin was caring for a small group of children out of their apartment, which was located nearby the Lewins in student housing. The two couples became fast friends.

Despite the financial stress Danny and Anne faced, Anne never lost confidence in Danny's potential for success. She didn't know anything about algorithms or computer science, but she did know her husband was brilliant and determined. In a documentary tribute to Danny, Anne recalled a conversation she once had with him in their apartment in Haifa, where Danny kept a big, bulky personal computer that he loved to program. At the time, the World Wide Web had just made its debut, and it was unclear to most people what the impact of this newfangled technology would be. But Anne said Danny had a clear idea of its potential, explaining excitedly that the Internet would allow her to use a computer in Israel to access information from a library at Harvard University. Anne said she expressed her amazement, but added that it sounded complicated. Danny replied: "It is complicated. But can you imagine the possibilities? Can you imagine what we'll be able to do if someone makes it easy?"

Publish or perish. It's a well-known saying at the nation's best universities, one that sums up the fear among research-oriented graduate students that failure to publish in scholarly journals means academic doom.

By late fall, Lewin was beginning to feel the pressure. Salil Vadhan and Amit Sahai had already produced and published an impressive paper. But Lewin and his three writing partners—Eric Lehman, Rina Panigrahy, and Matthew Levine—were stuck. "We didn't feel like we were having much success," recalled Lehman.

Their focus was still on using math to relieve the congestion plaguing the complex architecture of the Internet. Specifically, they were still searching for a solution to the the problem of the World Wide Wait. Tim Berners-Lee had pushed to the fore of the theory group's work. Under the supervision of Tom Leighton and fellow LCS professor David Karger—an award-winning computer scientist with an expertise in applied algorithms—Lewin, Lehman, Panigrahy, and Levine were trying to improve on one of the existing approaches to hot spots, called "caching." As described earlier, caching allows for much faster delivery of Web pages to users because it skips over the numerous routers and transition points that form the Internet. Moving data over the Internet, such as downloading Web pages, tends to be a highly repetitive process. For each object on a page (such as pictures, text, logos and ads, etc.) multiple round trips are required between the server and the user's browser. Considering that the average Web page contains anywhere from ten to thirty objects and that the server might be thousands of miles from the requesting computer, it's easy to understand why slowdowns are a problem.

There are several ways to cache content, and all of them involve high-level math and engineering. That's because, to function efficiently, caches need to "think." An efficient caching system is able to refresh or change content so as to reflect changes to the Web pages. It is also able to understand the construction of Web pages so it can refresh only the objects that change often. Caching is accomplished through servers, which are positioned between the source of the content and the user requesting it.

Lewin scrutinized the most sophisticated math underlying caching software and eventually created the foundation for a new Web caching technique called "consistent hashing." Hashing (not to be confused with "caching") is a method of accessing data by assigning it a set of unique numbers. Hashing schemes work well when the number of servers is known and fixed. But on the Internet, where the number of servers is always in flux, it's relatively useless—unless particular algorithms instruct the servers on how to readjust their respective loads. With this in mind, Lewin set out to develop a new set of algorithms that that would claim something no other caching strategy could: fault-tolerance.

A useful, non-mathematical metaphor for understanding consistent hashing is the storage of files. Say you are given a task which, at the outset, appears easy: to store a large stack of files in several cabinets in some particular order, a system you can remember later when you want to retrieve a particular file. Obviously, there are several ways the files can be organized. One of the most obvious is by alphabet—the A's on one shelf, the B's on the next, and so on. This strategy functions well until there is a surplus of A files. Suddenly that cabinet is full, and you're left with no logical place to store them. If they go into the cabinet for the B files, the B's might get squeezed out, meaning some B's would have to be shifted to the C cabinet, some C's would move to the D cabinet, and so on. To make matter worse, what if two of the filing cabinets break, forcing you to remove all of the files they contain and stuff them into the cabinets with extra room? There would no longer be a clear destination for any one file. The system, once working smoothly, now becomes messy. Using algorithms, consistent hashing offered a way of organizing files—or any kind of data—optimally. Consistent hashing meant that when a new "cabinet" was added or a new set of files was introduced, they would be spread evenly and consistently across said "cabinets."

Eric Lehman distinctly recalled the day Lewin shared this new idea with him and just how insecure he was about its potential. "We were walking together across campus and Danny was kind of down on his research," said Lehman. "He told me about consistent hashing, and I'll never forget it because he said, 'Consistent hashing is a pathetic idea, but it's *my* idea.'"

Mathematicians often describe proofs, theorems, and algorithms using the same adjectives one might use to describe a woman or a work of art. Sometimes their work is elegant and beautiful. In rare cases, it is stunning. According to Lehman, Lewin originally thought his idea of consistent hashing was simplistic and impractical: "He was worried it was small and worthless, just something cute." To clarify, in mathematical jargon, "cute" means the work looks good on the surface, but lacks utility and mathematical sophistication. Lewin and Lehman thought they had a cute idea to work with, but they knew they needed to improve it somehow. Lehman, though, was uncertain if this could be done: "Honestly, we didn't know very much about how the Internet worked at the time, and we were struggling with how to convert this real world problem of file storage into a mathematical model. On paper, our mathematical model didn't seem that realistic, so the whole thing seemed kind of shaky to me."

However pathetic Lewin himself felt it to be, however, he did believe consistent hashing might have some practical utility. "In that same conversation in which he called it pathetic," Lehman added, "I remember Danny saying he really thought something like this could exist." With this in mind, Lewin and Lehman forged ahead, and, at some point, decided to present their research their adviser, David Karger. A brilliant mathematician, Karger earned his PhD at Harvard. Nonetheless, Lewin and Lehman both found him difficult to interact with because he was often prickly and dismissive of their ideas. Consequently, they approached Karger with some apprehension. According to Lehman, the meeting did not go well. Karger didn't think Lewin's idea had legs, so to speak, and even referred to it as insignificant. Lehman reported that he and Lewin were deflated: "It was really upsetting, and it almost pushed us over the edge."[4]

However frustrated he might have been, though, Lewin wasn't about to let the idea of consistent hashing go. He still had faith in it, and told Lehman he'd will it into greatness if he had to. But first they needed a second opinion, and there was no question who they would approach to get it: Tom Leighton.

If there exists a mathematical concept that is as logical and precise as it is confusing and abstract, it is the algorithm. The mere mention of the term has the power to illicit a baffled shrug or a shudder in those who are not mathematically inclined. What, exactly, is an algorithm? When posed to a dozen people, the question is likely to produce a dozen different replies. The answer, however, is almost deceptively simple. An algorithm is a precise, finite set of instructions for carrying out a procedure or solving a problem. And although an algorithm is a mathematical concept, the finite instructions themselves (or, in layman's terms, "recipes") needn't involve math. We use algorithms almost daily for tasks as varied as baking a cake, driving from one place to another, looking up a word in the dictionary, or filing taxes. Algorithms are the methodologies we use to solve problems, and they govern everyday life.

To walk through a basic example of an algorithm outside of computing, consider planning a trip from one city to another. There are several ways you can make the trip, and each one can be mapped using a basic algorithm. In scenario one, you get in your car and drive from City A to City B. In scenario two, you take a taxi to the train station and board a train from City A to City B. And in yet another scenario, you take a taxi to the airport and catch a flight from City A to City B. These are three algorithms with three very different ways of accomplishing the exact same goal. The same is true for computer programming. Often, many different algorithms can be used to accomplish a task with the same end result, but each algorithm results in varying degrees of time or cost or both.

Why, then, is there so often an aura of complexity or mystery surrounding the algorithm? The answer is ironically simple: the algorithms worth talking about, those that have accomplished great tasks, are not easy to follow. And in computer science, they are often so difficult and mathematically rigorous that they seem almost illusory to anyone outside of the field. Computer programmers use these types of algorithms to instruct machines to execute certain functions in the most efficient way possible. They're still step-by-step recipes with an end result, but, in computer science, the steps to reach that end result contain the symbols and language of computer programming: nodes, inputs, outputs, and variables. If you don't speak the language, it becomes an abstraction. In his book *The Advent of the Algorithm*, author David Berlinski summed up the elusive nature of the algorithm as "an abstract instrument of coordination, supplying procedural means to various ends…algorithms, like thoughts, reside in a world beyond time."[5]

Notably, algorithms used in early computer science are practically synonymous with Alan Turing, who preceded Tom Leighton at Princeton by four decades. Turing was a pioneer in many fields, including information theory, mathematics, and cryptography. But Turing is best known for the machine bearing his name—the "Turing machine"—an imaginary problem-solving device that existed only on paper. Presaging the invention of the modern computer, Turing designed a virtual construct that could store and run sets of instructions, or algorithms. He dreamed up the idea before real, programmable computing devices existed. It was so revolutionary that it sparked a new era of modern computing driven by algorithms and rigorous mathematical proofs.[6]

Algorithms have been used for historic breakthroughs in all areas of science, from computational biology to quantum computing. But they occupy an exclusive place in the field of computer science because they are finite and discreet. As Berlinski explained, they "specify only a series of numbers, the conversion of those numbers into a pattern for the mathematician to decide." As computer scientists like to say, a computer is a storyteller and algorithms are its tales. In the eye of certain beholders, an algorithm can be beautiful. Francis Sullivan, an American theologian, likened algorithms to literature: "For me, great algorithms are the poetry of computation. Just like verse, they can be terse, allusive, dense, and even mysterious. But once unlocked, they cast a brilliant new light on some aspect of computing."

The most influential twentieth-century advocate for the power of algorithms in computer science was Stanford professor Donald Knuth. Knuth was born in Milwaukee, Wisconsin, where his father owned a small printing business and taught bookkeeping. Knuth's intelligence made him a standout from an early age, both for his academic acumen and for the sometimes peculiar ways he applied it. In eighth grade, he won a contest by finding over 4,500 words that could be formed from the letters in "Ziegler's Giant Bar"; the judges themselves had only about 2,500 words on their master list. In 1957, during his senior year, Knuth won the Westinghouse Talent Search, the same scholarship awarded to Leighton in 1974. He hoped to pursue a career in music, but his plans changed when the Case Institute (later Case Western Reserve) offered him a full scholarship in physics. He soon realized that he loved math more than physics, specifically the area of discreet mathematics. In 1963, he earned a PhD in mathematics from the California Institute of Technology and began working there as associate professor.

Knuth argued passionately for the marriage of math and computer science, based on his firm belief that the two fields could do nothing but enrich each other. It wasn't a popular stance, particularly to traditional mathematicians. But Knuth knew that, at its highest levels, math—specifically the study of algorithms—could be applied to our understanding and creation of computers. Computer science was just emerging, with caution, onto the scene. Knuth wrote: "It was a totally new field, with no real identity. And the standard of available publications was not that high. A lot of the papers coming out were quite simply wrong.... So one of my motivations was to put straight a story that had been very badly told."[7]

Knuth authored a seven-volume tome that became the bible of computer science: *The Art of Computer Programming* was first published in 1968. One of its first lessons is on hashing.

By the time Lewin and Lehman arranged a meeting with Tom Leighton, though, they hadn't gained a great deal of confidence in consistent hashing. Leighton remembered the two of them appearing slightly embarrassed when they approached him for feedback. "They presented it almost as an afterthought," Leighton said. "They told me about the concept in what was an apologetic way."

Almost instantly, however, Leighton saw something significant. "I thought, oh, my goodness because they had a whole bunch of stuff—proof of this, proof of that, all these things. I said, 'Wow, that's a gem; that's really cool [and] you wouldn't expect you could do this.'" Leighton had never thought about hashing the way Lewin and Lehman presented it. In fact, their approach seemed almost impossible. But there it was in front of him, stapled neatly and sitting on his desk. Lewin didn't yet have the deep proofs, but he had something. And to Leighton, it was beautiful.

"I remember being struck," Leighton confessed. "It wasn't a tour de force technically, and in mathematics you often want to have that kind of thing, but it was just—I thought it was elegant and fundamental, and I remember just appreciating the beauty, the elegance, and what I thought was going to be the importance of it."

According to Leighton, the potential power of consistent hashing was rooted in its simplicity. Lewin had taken a succinct problem— one that was easy to state but seemingly impossible to solve—and created a solution so simple and elegant it was almost...obvious. "Mathematics has a lot of examples like this, where you could take a thousand people and they wouldn't be able to solve the problem, but they could all quickly agree when you show them the solution that it's easy," Leighton clarified. "It's a weird thing, to be convinced that a solution works is much different than coming up with one."

At the time, Leighton looked at Lewin and Lehman and exclaimed, "You've done it. This is really important, and you've got to give it a name and state the definition of the problem because this sounds useful."

It was the beginning of the end of the World Wide Wait.

CHAPTER 4

May Madness

"A significant invention must be startling,
unexpected. It must come to a world that is not
prepared for it. If the world were prepared for it,
it would not be much of an invention."

— DR. EDWIN LAND,
Polaroid founder, 1975 interview in Forbes *magazine*

Like so many graduate students living on meager stipends, Danny and Anne were struggling financially. Naturally, their student loans were mounting. To ease the strain, Lewin took a job sweeping the halls of their apartment complex in exchange for a discount on rent. But life with two kids meant unforeseen and often unremitting expenses. Some weeks, in an exercise of frugality, they cut the more costly items, like meat, from their grocery list. Friends recalled Lewin wrestling with the seemingly small decision of whether or not to replace one of the boy's lunchboxes, which had been dented. Lewin had always been resourceful, taking on a newspaper route in Colorado on his own initiative when he was in the fourth grade. In Israel, he always found ways to financially emancipate himself from his parents. He worked at a pizza parlor as a teenager, and later, in exchange for a membership at Samson's gym, he took a job cleaning the locker rooms. But now the demands of school and home didn't allow him the time to take on any more odd jobs—and the money woes were keeping him and Anne up at night. Lewin needed funds, and he needed them fast.

Lewin's neighbor and close friend Preetish Nijhawan, a second-year student at MIT's Sloan School of Business, knew how stressed Danny and Anne were. Nijhawan had a family of his own, and, as mentioned earlier, his wife Shirin pulled in extra money by babysitting a few kids during the week, including Eitan and Itamar Lewin. One afternoon in 1997, Nijhawan came to Lewin with an idea—one he felt could be their ticket to riches. It was a business contest hosted by the students at the Sloan School. And unlike other student-organized events, this one—called the MIT $50K Entrepreneurship Competition—could mean real money. Nijhawan, who formerly worked for Intel, understood Lewin's core work on consistent hashing, and saw the possibility of applying it to the Internet. Over lunch with Lewin, Nijhawan proposed an idea: he and Lewin should build a business plan out of the research Lewin was doing with Tom Leighton and enter the 50K. Lewin was unsure, until Nijhawan told him about the prize money. The winner of the contest, he said, received a staggering sum: $50,000. To Lewin, this sounded like all the money in the world. He didn't need any more convincing. He and Nijhawan talked it over, and decided that if consistent hashing had the potential to improve the speed and efficiency of the Internet, it had the potential to inspire a winning business plan—one that would sell software (powered by complex math and consistent hashing) to companies on the promise that it would change the way they delivered content on the Internet.

That same afternoon, Lewin and Nijhawan went directly to Leighton's office hoping to convince him to join their just-formed business team. Leighton was surprised. He had a bit of business experience selling some of his patents to Polaroid but never planned to start up anything of his own, even on paper. "Danny and I had been proving theorems, but we hadn't been thinking at all about a business aspect," Leighton said. "I might have been the most unlikely person in the world to start a company." In addition, he wasn't entirely certain that, where he saw beauty, others would see potential. He also worried because, at his own urging, Lewin had submitted, to no avail, an initial paper on consistent hashing to a renowned conference called the Symposium on Discreet Algorithms. In the rejection notice, the conference committee members stated that they didn't think consistent hashing had any hope of being useful.

But Lewin managed to persuade Leighton, with his characteristic zeal, that they had nothing to lose. It was just an academic exercise; at least, that's one way Leighton could look at it. By the time Lewin and Nijhawan left Leighton's office, he was on board.

The first challenge in the lead up to the 50K was the business plan itself. Lewin and Leighton had some great ideas, but nothing close to a compelling proposition for a startup. "Designing a system was a very different endeavor for us," said Leighton. "It was still on paper, but it wasn't going to be mathematical anymore." Lewin went to the library and checked out a stack of books on business plans and startups. He then passed them on to Leighton, insisting that he read them, too. Bonnie Berger said she'll never forget her husband arriving home with volumes of instructional manuals and staying up two nights in a row reading them. "They really had no idea what they were doing," commented Berger. "I remember Tom started getting really interested in this contest with Danny and I remember it evolving, and I remember Danny would be coming by with all his energy and sucking Tom into it even more every time." Leighton, though, remembered being sucked in willingly and marveling at Lewin's spirited approach to the contest. "It was through that process that I really got the impression that Danny had tremendous drive and no fear," recalled Leighton. "If he didn't know something, he'd go learn it."

Together, they decided their business would sell boxes equipped with their technology, rooted in a set of algorithms, to Internet Service Providers. The ISPs would then sell it as a service—one to speed up the delivery content online—to their existing customers, the content providers. Consistent hashing would drive the software, but it only merited one line in the business plan, which said the technology would "apply a set of algorithms that allow the data storage and retrieval to occur quickly and efficiently without the need for a central directory." They called the company Cachet Technologies, a play on "caching" and what they hoped would be their company's winning reputation.

The MIT $50K Entrepreneurship Competition has been called the "Granddaddy" of multiple business plan competitions that now exist at universities around the country. Its origins date back to 1989, when students from MIT's engineering school and Sloan School decided to join forces for an annual entrepreneurship challenge that could give rise to new businesses. With the support of John Preston, the director of MIT's Technology Licensing Office, the organizers raised enough money that opening year to offer a $10,000 prize to the winning team in order to file a patent.

Over the next few years, the competition morphed into something much greater than its prize money. It became an opportunity to shake hands and exchange business cards with potential investors who scouted each year's entry list in search of the next big thing. It was the chance to open doors and even gain a fast track to capital and media attention. Although it took place in an academic setting, the MIT competition was no longer an academic exercise. Five years earlier, Michael Cassidy, a student in MIT's aerospace engineering program, took his first-place business plan for a software company and formed Stylus Innovation, Inc., in Cambridge. He then sold it for $12.9 million in cash, becoming a millionaire at age thirty-three. By 1998, the year Lewin and his team planned to enter, the contest had spawned the creation of thirty companies with an aggregate market value of over seventy million.[1] Veterans of the contest included Lexicus, which developed handwriting recognition software (bought by Motorola in 1993), Firefly Network, which created the first online music community (acquired by Microsoft in 1998), and Silicon Spice, which created semiconductors for telecommunications companies (acquired by Broadcom in 2000 in a deal worth $1 billion).[2]

These success stories, combined with the gathering force of the technology boom, amplified the excitement about the contest in the months leading up to the application deadline. Its nickname had become the "Who wants to be a zillionaire?" competition, and the early buzz suggested the 50k was poised to launch a big hit that year. Meanwhile, Lewin was beginning to feel like Cachet's idea had real traction.

To add weight to the credentials of their team, Lewin turned to friend Jonathan Seelig. Seelig was in his first semester of business school at Sloan, and, like Lewin, he had moved to Cambridge directly from Israel where he had been working for the Israel-based ECI Telecom. A graduate of Stanford with a degree in physics, Seelig was well on his way to a high-tech career in Israel when he decided to apply to MIT for graduate school. "To me, MIT was the place where you had the greatest creation of technological innovation and the greatest opportunity to build things from it," said Seelig, who has a lanky, tall frame and longish brown hair that he tucks behind his ears when he talks. "The idea of being in a place with such academic and intellectual ability was exciting to me."

Seelig had some money saved from his work in Israel, and was looking forward to a few more years of the student life. He rented a one-bedroom bachelor pad in Central Square, right between the campuses of MIT and Harvard. Lewin was one of dozens of new friends Seelig made that fall in Cambridge, but he and Lewin formed an instant kinship. "My first impression of him was of this forceful, passionate guy," Seelig recalled. "I was struck by how 'present' he was. Whenever you were talking about something, Danny was really there, listening carefully."

Having worked in the telecomm industry, Seelig was well aware of the challenges to scaling the Internet. When he sat down for one of his first meetings with Lewin in Leighton's office, he hadn't read Lewin's work on consistent hashing. All he knew was that the two of them had come up with some sets of algorithms they thought would be effective to store content on the Internet in the optimal way. "At the time, thinking about how to make the Internet work better seemed like a terrific idea," noted Seelig.

December 1997 marked the warm-up round of the 50K, a smaller competition leading up to the main event that would be held in the following spring. In the application materials, the organizers stated that the warm-up round, while not required, is the ideal opportunity to get a sense of the strengths and weaknesses of your plan. The Cachet team—which included Lewin, Leighton and Nijhawan—entered with a three-page business plan titled "Scalable Caching and Replication Solutions for High Bandwidth Applications."

On December 10, the judges announced the most innovative business plans of the warm-up round in ten separate categories. Cachet took home the software and media prize, which came with a $100 check (the early round had a cash prize of $1,000, which was split among the ten category winners). The win offered the three of them great hope that they had a shot at taking the $50K. Unfortunately for Lewin, however, the warm-up round came with an unexpected realization: the winner of the main contest would not, in fact, take home $50K. Instead, the prize money would be split between the two top winners, and the bulk of it had to be spent on startup costs. Still, a win would mean money in the bank. What's more, it could mean the launch of a successful startup. And in the late 1990s, the fastest road to riches was a dot-com sensation. So by the start of the New Year, Lewin began putting together a more formidable team for the official 50K competition, starting with Seelig, whom he convinced to come on board.

In September, Lewin sent an e-mail to best friend Marco Greenberg, in which he wrote: "I have a great idea to talk to you about—one that could make us big $$$." Born in Hollywood and raised in

Brentwood and Beverly Hills, Greenberg, whose father was a prominent Los Angeles architect and self-made millionaire, was a natural born networker with a Rolodex of wealthy friends of the family to tap into. Greenberg wasn't a mathematician, but he knew Lewin well enough to understand that whatever he was doing, there was a good chance it could be big. "I actually failed trigonometry at Beverly Hills High School in the twelfth grade, whereas Danny was probably mastering trig when he was in the fourth grade," admitted Greenberg. "In that way, we were sort of an odd couple. When he'd show me his math textbooks, I'd say, 'Danny, you know the only thing I understand in this is the first sentence of the foreword. Everything else, you lost me.'"

Lewin and Greenberg's friendship, formed in the crucible of Israel, had not flagged a bit since the summer of 1986 when the two first met. Although they were both tough guys with some Israeli machismo, Lewin and Greenberg connected on a profound level as friends, with a mutual trust and respect evident in their regular correspondence (by postal mail until the mid-1990s, when they began using e-mail). Greenberg said that Lewin knew him better than almost anyone. Lewin knew him well enough to understand—based on nothing more than a few straightforward words—when Greenberg needed a friend.

A year after Lewin moved from Israel to Cambridge and Greenberg helped him through that tough transition, Greenberg made a tough move of his own from Israel to New York. And for the first time in his life, Greenberg experienced a fleeting, but frightening, bout of depression stemming from his departure from Israel. During this time, he called Lewin in Cambridge and let his guard down. "I didn't get all into it or anything, I just let him know that I was depressed and having a hard time," Greenberg later recounted. He didn't have to say anything more. That weekend, Lewin traveled to New York and arrived at Greenberg's apartment just to "hang out" for a few days. Greenberg said, "He did it to say, 'Hey, I'm here for you.'" Although he was the son of a psychiatrist, Lewin typically shied away from any kind of "psychobabble," often poking fun at the question: "How does that make you feel?" Given this, Greenberg was particularly grateful that Lewin came calling on him at a low point. "Danny's sensitive and empathetic side was surprisingly advanced for a commando turned computer scientist," Greenberg noted wryly.

Although Greenberg had his own business to grow, if there was a chance for Cachet to succeed, he wanted to be on board. "I always appreciated Danny's keen mathematical mind, which obviously influenced his thinking in general. And I remember once, when he was in the early stages of the contest, he told me, 'This is going to be so big that you're going to have so many clients of your own because they will come to you knowing you worked with us. Your business is going to be huge!'"

One of the first connections Greenberg made for the Cachet team was a young businessman named Randall Kaplan. Kaplan graduated from law school, but then jumped to the business world when he landed a job at the asset management firm SunAmerica, now a subsidiary of American International Group (AIG). By age twenty-seven, Kaplan was reporting directly to Eli Broad, the billionaire philanthropist who was then the company's CEO. But Kaplan was eager to rise upward and considering investing in a business of his own. When he heard about Cachet Technologies from Greenberg, he was intrigued enough to contact Lewin directly, and before he knew it he was working with the Cachet team—putting his legal and business background to use in negotiations with MIT's Technology Licensing Office to get the best possible deal in the event the company took off. Lewin was happy to have Kaplan on board. On January 8, 1998, Lewin wrote an e-mail to Greenberg thanking him for the connections to potential funders, including Kaplan. "You're a fuckin' stud!" he wrote, adding that they would soon be "home free to zillionaire land."

Lewin loved the word "zillionaire." To him, it was just another expression of the kind of magnitude with which he worked to define his life. But the fact was, the business plan was just one of the many things Lewin was juggling at the time. With no guarantee that Cachet would go beyond a few pieces of paper, let alone bring him great wealth, Lewin continued to focus on his master's thesis and coursework with Leighton. On January 18, he e-mailed Greenberg to share his hopes for Cachet:

> I am really not worried about getting money for Cachet. The main issue on my mind is how to set up Cachet so I don't have to leave MIT. This is very important to me. If I cannot see a way, I'm going to sell the patent and make off with as much as I can. The point is that, 20 years from now—even if I am a zillionaire—I would not forgive myself for leaving the PhD [program].

Then there were his obligations at home, where Anne was doing double time caring for Eitan and Itamar during Danny's long days on campus and late nights at LCS. Even when he was home, Lewin was often occupied. On January 26, 1998, he had to stay home with Eitan, who was sick, so Anne could go to work. Still, he managed to fire off an e-mail to Greenberg with an update on the 50K competition:

> Our main advantage (which has not been proven yet) over the competition is that our product is suitable for deployment over a wide network, and not at a single point in the network. Without going into details, this is what BOTH the telephone and cable companies may want to do. I still don't have all the data, but Tom is pushing ahead strongly. We will see what happens.

In March of 1998, Lewin asked Greenberg to come to Cambridge so he could introduce him to Leighton, the smartest man he'd ever met. Greenberg went willingly and became awed by the obvious chemistry between the two. "Danny called me and told me he'd met this great professor and they had this idea, and it was clear after I schlepped up to Cambridge for this meeting that Tom was at the pinnacle of Danny's professional and personal worldview," said Greenberg. "I completely believed in the two of them."

Greenberg took charge of publicity for the fledgling business, and his first task was to rename it. Although Greenberg had come up with the name Cachet Technologies, he thought it lacked punch—particularly compared with the much sexier dot-com monikers that defined the times, like Amazon.com and eBay. Besides, they weren't promising cachet; they were promising something fast and intelligent. Greenberg spent countless hours thinking up potential names, even on napkins over dinner with his girlfriend: Bonzai? Fast Lane? Out of Bounds?

Nothing seemed to stick. And nothing had the exotic allure of, say, the hot new startup Inktomi. The California software company created a new standard of cool when they chose Inktomi (pronounced "INK-tuh-me"), derived from a Native American legend about a crafty spider. Lewin suggested Hawaiian words, which resonated with Greenberg, who had a family connection to the island state. He drafted a few lists of potential monikers, and, before sending them to Lewin and Leighton, Greenberg called a Hawaiian travel and media contact to make sure he had the most accurate definition for each word—and that none of them had any "unpleasant" connotations or double meanings that he should be aware of. After hearing back, he sent his top choices to Lewin and Leighton. They included: *Ao* (world), *Kulako* (island style), *Owiwi* (fast), and *Akamai*. Leighton sent a reply to Greenberg with a unanimous decision: *Akamai*.

Akamai. Hawaiian term.
Smart, clever, expert; smartness, skill.

Cf. akeakamai. *Na 'olelo akamai a Kolomana*
The proverbs of Solomon
(pronounced Ah-kuh-mi)

It wasn't easy to pronounce, but it was hip, pithy, and unique.

By April of 1998, with a business plan in the works and their sights set on the 50K competition, the Akamai team was moving so fast that Lewin was in a state of disbelief. Early hype was building around some of the 50K teams, some of which were rumored to have already secured venture capital support. Lewin was starting to think they had a real shot at winning, or at least getting some funding. In an e-mail to Greenberg, Lewin expressed his hope that Akamai would have seed money by the start of the summer, adding, "I can't believe this is happening!"

And it wasn't—yet. The 50K competition was still a month away, and Akamai needed to finalize its business plan. By this time, the Akamai team had collectively recruited enough prestigious supporters that, on paper, they appeared credible. On the technical side, in addition to Lewin and Leighton, the team now included MIT Professor David Karger (with whom Lewin had made peace), Bill Bogstad, a veteran network developer, Robert Thau from Apache, programming protégés Alex Sherman and Yoav Yerushalmi, and ten students from LCS. On the business side, in addition to Jonathan Seelig, Preetish Nijhawan, and Marco Greenberg, they added David Crosbie, from Sitara Networks, and Steve Papa, a Harvard Business School graduate from Inktomi. Their advisors included the legendary Michael Dertouzos, director of LCS, Albert Vezza, the founder and chairman of W3C, former Sun America businessman Randall Kaplan, Todd Dagres and Scott Tobin, shrewd investors with Battery Ventures, Sean Dalton of Harvard Business School, and Steve Bochner, attorney at Wilson Sonsini Goodrich & Rosati. It was, in Lewin's mind, a winning team.

At the end of April, Lewin submitted a thirty-eight-page entry to the 50K, with the cover: "Akamai, Global Hosting Servers, Changing the Way Content is Distributed Through the Internet." Akamai, according to the plan, would enable ISPs to host content at thousands of locations worldwide with the flip of a switch, allowing their Web sites to withstand flash crowds, serve up fresh content including graphics and multimedia, and reduce the cost of bandwidth. It was a plan on paper; far from a reality. But at a time when top engineers at supersites were working around the clock to improve the performance of the Internet, it was a promising one.

At MIT, the month of the 50K competition was called May Madness because it garnered the intensity and tension of a professional sports draft. Investors and business executives were already circling the Sloan School like buzzards, collecting early intelligence about the most anticipated teams of the year. At final count, the 50K had eighty-four entries—the largest number since the first contest in 1990—in categories including biotech, media and software, computer hardware, and services and consumer products. The twenty-four-person panel of judges was formidable, with big names such as Mitch Kapor, the founder of Lotus Development Corp., J. William Poduska Sr., founder of both Prime Computer and Apollo Computer, and Mark Gorenberg, an MIT graduate and managing director of the San Francisco firm Hummer Winblad Venture Partners.[3]

The official 50K presentations took place on May 5, 1998 in a small forum that included only the judges and the competing teams. Akamai took to the stage, but much to the surprise of everyone familiar with the team, Lewin was absent. Everyone knew Professor Leighton would hang back—he often did, preferring to let Lewin do the talking. But no one understood, in that moment, why Lewin was not presenting his grand idea. Instead, Lewin, Leighton, Kaplan, and Seelig were standing in the back of the auditorium. In their place was advisor David Crosbie, an Oxford-educated engineer who had only recently joined the team. "Danny thought it was better to have the business guy up there," said Seelig. Crosbie, who worked at the lofty Sitara Networks, had the stage. Yet members of the audience said it was clear from the start that he lacked the passion to put on the hard sell. Crosbie also made some unfortunate choices, like the decision to use a ball as a prop, which he tossed into the audience to demonstrate the pattern of data through routers. Noticeably perspiring and ill at ease, Crosbie presented a series of Power Point slides that formed Akamai's elevator pitch. They contained the following highlights:

CACHET: Content providers—e.g., CNN, L. L. Bean—need to attract customers to their site…and keep them there. This requires fast, easy, reliable access, personalized content, fancy graphics/multimedia. But ISPs today cannot give content providers the quality of service that they need. Result: The World Wide Wait.

PROBLEM ONE: Flash crowds. Content becomes unexpectedly popular and swamps both the server and network. Existing solution: design system for max load, which is too expensive and unpredictable. CNN's solution: remove all large content, which degrades the site quality and is an administrative nightmare.

PROBLEM TWO: Distance. Almost all users [are] distant from [a] central site, which costs money and takes time. One solution: Content Providers install servers at hosting farms (e.g. Digex, Exodus, UUNET) that are located near network access points—but these are still less than halfway to [the] user.

CURRENT TECHNOLOGY: Mirroring, which fully duplicates all content at a few locations, but is very expensive, limited in scale, and requires huge administrative overhead.

THE AKAMAI BREAKTHROUGH…Enables ISPs to host content at thousands of locations worldwide with the flip of a switch. This means: content is always near the user that wants it, intelligent replication handles flash crowds, content providers maintain control over their databases, content is always fresh, technology is transparent and implemented in the software, and it allows for enhanced graphics and multimedia and reduces bandwidth costs.

What the Akamai team didn't know at the time, however, was that asking Crosbie to present would prove a fatal misstep.

Mark Gorenberg of Hummer Winblad still remembers the presentation clearly; it was the only time in his four years of judging that he'd seen someone other than an MIT student on the competition's stage. "They decided that, in order to have a better chance of winning, they would let the boat's anchor, in venture parlance, make the presentation," said Gorenberg. "The judges who didn't know the company ahead of time didn't know what they were trying to do; it wasn't clear from the presentation. He (Crosbie) had a great resume, but he didn't really understand what they were doing."

Crosbie was no match for a few of the contestants who followed, particularly MIT graduate Mike Cassidy, who was entering the 50K for the second time as an advisor to Direct Hit, a company that would make software for Internet search engines. Cassidy's 1993 entry, Stylus Innovations, Inc., had made him a millionaire. This time, he was banking on Direct Hit—and his presentation was a sensation. The Akamai team left feeling uneasy. But if Lewin was anxious, he didn't show it.

The main event of the competition was held on May 6, 1998, before a large crowd of students and business folks who crammed into MIT's Kresge Auditorium. Bill Porter, a Sloan graduate who founded E*Trade, delivered the keynote address. Following this, the teams presented again before the crowd. This time, Seelig and Nijhawan made the pitch, and the reception was much more enthusiastic. "At that point, it was just theater; the die had been cast," remarked Seelig, referring to the fact that the Akamai team already knew, for a fact, they had not won.

In contrast to their losing performance the day before, Akamai made a lasting impression. "They blew it out of the water," said Gorenberg, who remembered being chased down the hall by investors asking him why the judges had not selected Akamai as the winner. One of them, Gorenberg recalled, was entrepreneur Alexander Vladimir D'Arbeloff, an MIT graduate who co-founded the Boston-based, high-tech company Teradyne and chaired the MIT Corporation. To this day, Gorenberg says the story of the Akamai 50K serves as a critical lesson for budding entrepreneurs: a startup's greatest weapon is often the passion of its founder.

At the end of the presentations, the judges spoke. For the first time in history, they said, "Our panel is deadlocked, and two teams will share the top prize." The judges continued: "And the winners are…Direct Hit, and Volunteer Community Connection!" Then they delivered the list of runners-up. "In third place…CarSoft, which will connect home computers with diagnostic tools in cars. In second place…SiliconTest, which will design cards for the testing of semiconductor chips. In third place…WeddingBell.com, which will register wedding gifts on the Internet…" By the time they announced Akamai, which took fifth place, it seemed no one was even listening.

The winning teams took home $30,000 each, after an anonymous donor fattened the prize money with a $20,000 check. The

CarSoft team took home a $10,000 prize. Then, in another unexpected turn, the Direct Hit team donated its $30,000 winnings to the other top two finalists after announcing they had received a commitment for $1.3 million in funding. The winners went on to launch successful businesses: Direct Hit was sold to Ask Jeeves for $507 million, and United Way acquired Volunteer Community Connection. The brains behind CarSoft, Diego Borrego, transformed the plan into Networkfleet, one of the most successful automotive technology companies.[4]

After almost a year of preparation and planning, the 50K loss proved a big blow to Lewin: "It was a slap in the face," Leighton recalled. "Danny didn't like losing." Lewin was also angry with himself for pushing Crosbie out as their front man. And, as Seelig noted, "Danny was at a low after 50K. But he wasn't as much down as he was pissed off, and I think that made him more selective about the team going forward, and more determined to make this work."

In retrospect, both Leighton and Seelig conceded that the judges were right: they hadn't deserved a win. Not because of Crosbie, but because their business plan, which positioned the company as a vendor of software to ISPs, was fundamentally flawed. The software segment was already crowded with potential competitors, and their technology seemed better suited to something larger scale. "I don't think, at heart, we disagreed with the assessment," Leighton admitted. "We realized where we were deficient. We didn't think our business plan was ready for primetime or that it could really work."

Lewin didn't have time to linger on the loss, however. He had a master's thesis to deliver, which included two new algorithms he still believed had the potential to change the delivery of content on the Internet. Leighton, concerned that his supervision of Lewin's thesis could appear as a conflict of interest considering their collaboration on Akamai, suggested that Lewin secure a co-signer on the paper. He needed someone whose name would carry with it a seal of approval, signifying that his work was academically rigorous. The best person for this was obvious: Professor Karger. Lewin agreed, and put aside his earlier displeasure with Karger in order to deliver the best possible thesis.

On May 22, 1998, Lewin delivered his thesis, titled: "Consistent Hashing and Random Trees: Algorithms for Caching in Distributed Networks." In it, he developed what he called "the algorithmic foundation of a large-scale distributed caching system for the World Wide Web." The algorithmic foundation was consistent hashing, which Lewin combined with a data replication technique called "random trees" to come up with a way to allow a large network of caches to cooperate without overloading any one server. The system would remain robust, he wrote, even when overloaded and in a constant state of flux: "Servers can become swamped unexpectedly and without any prior notice. For example, a site mentioned as the 'cool site of the day' on the evening news may have to deal with a ten thousand-fold increase in traffic during the next day. This is known as the "flash crowd" phenomenon and the server in such a case is called a 'hot spot.'"

In the acknowledgments, Lewin thanked Leighton, then added: "Most importantly, I would like to thank my lovely wife and kids for being there." The paper garnered him the Joseph Morris Levin Award for the best Master Works oral thesis presentation, an academic honor awarded to just a few MIT students a year. Despite his academic home run, though, Lewin couldn't let go of Akamai and the belief that it could build a better, faster Internet.[5]

A week after the 50K loss, on his twenty-eighth birthday, Lewin sent Greenberg a contemplative e-mail from Toronto, where he was presenting research on "Probabilistically checkable proofs" at an academic conference:

Silicon valley makes money on air...There are many in this business who become horrendously wealthy AND THEY DON'T EVEN HAVE

A PRODUCT OR CLIENT!!!!! ...You may say—so [what,] that is great—you do nothing and become a zillionaire. Unfortunately this is not the case. The main thing you do have to do is dedicate yourself to telling lies for a number of years and to spreading bullshit for many, many years. Some people are comfortable with this as long as the payoff at the end is high enough. I am not. The plan is to become a successful company in the right way. That is: have a product, have a market, and have customers who are buying your product. In order to do this well, we have to focus on building the technology and not on fundraising.

Toward the close of the e-mail, Lewin also expressed hope that once he got the company off the ground, venture capitalists would take over the bulk of the work: "This will allow me to return to my family life and to see my wonderful kids and wife," he wrote. "That's something far more valuable than millions $'s!!!"

Lewin didn't need millions. But he desperately needed some money in the bank. The financial woes he and Anne faced were only worsening; they were close to broke. Lewin had his long-term hopes pinned on Akamai, but the company still existed only on paper. He needed a summer income, and the best prospect came in an offer from the algorithms research group at Bell Laboratories, owned by Alcatel-Lucent in Berkeley Heights, New Jersey. It was a coveted position for any graduate student: an internship that paid in both prestige and money. It was also one Lewin had been hoping for, despite the distance it would create between him and his family, who would have to remain in Cambridge for the summer.

Lewin first learned about work at the legendary labs earlier that year, when two of his classmates, Anna Lysyanskaya and Yevgeniy Dodis, secured internships of their own. By the time he got around to applying, however, rumor had it that all the paid positions had been filled. When he heard this, Lewin immediately e-mailed Dodis, pleading with him to ask the scientist in charge of the internship program to make an exception:

FROM: Daniel Lewin <danl@theory.lcs.mit.edu>
TO: yevgen@theory.lcs.mit.edu
SUBJECT: Re: elementary question

Tell him that the life of a man with two children has been devastated by this (decision not to hire more students)—he cannot justify this pain and suffering that has been cast down upon me.... Oy! It is a sad story... So sad... That surely will convince him!

Fortunately, no one needed convincing. Lewin got the job, and in June of that year, he left Anne and the boys in Cambridge and moved into a shared student apartment in New Brunswick, New Jersey, with three MIT classmates for the summer. It could not have been easy on Anne, juggling schoolwork and parenting Eitan and Itamar alone. But they needed the money, and Lewin promised to make the long drive back to Cambridge every weekend to be with them.

Danny Lewin as an infant with his mother, Peggy.
Lewin family

Lewin with his younger brother, Michael.
Lewin family

Lewin as a young
teenager in Israel.
Lewin family

Lewin working out at
Samson's gym in Jerusalem.
Lewin family

Lewin as a soldier in the
Israel Defense Forces;
he served as an officer
in the army's most elite
counterterrorism unit,
Sayeret Matkal.
Lewin family

Marco Greenberg (left), and Lewin by the Western Wall in the city of Jerusalem, where the two first met and became best friends.
Marco Greenberg

Danny and Anne on their wedding day—August 20, 1991—in Jerusalem. The pair wed in a small ceremony attended by family and a few friends.
Anne Lewin Arundale

Anne and Danny with their two sons, baby Itamar (with Anne) and Eitan (with Danny) on a trip to Israel in the late '90s.
Anne Lewin Arundale

Tom Leighton and Lewin in front of one of the white boards they used to draft algorithms at MIT's Lab for Computer Science.
Chia Messina

Lewin and Leighton (with his back to the camera) huddled with co-workers for a meeting at Akamai in 1999.
Akamai

(From left) Leighton, Lewin, Paul Sagan, and Jonathan Seelig in 1999, shortly after Akamai was founded.
Akamai

Lewin and Paul Sagan at a data center at Boeing Field in Seattle, using a tool kit to reassemble Akamai servers that crashed during the company's first month of business.
Paul Sagan

Akamai Technologies headquarters in Cambridge, Massachusetts. *Akamai*

Akamai's Network Operations Control Center, from which the company has a bird's eye view of global Internet traffic. *Akamai*

Lewin on one of the many motorcycles he purchased with his newfound wealth after Akamai's successful public offering in October 1999.
Laura Malo

An iconic shot of Lewin and Leighton on the steps of MIT's great dome in 1999, just after the formation of Akamai.
The Boston Globe

Danny Lewin's name on the 9/11 Memorial in New York, at the site where the World Trade towers once stood.
Molly Knight Raskin

CHAPTER 5

Secret Sauce

"We can't solve problems by using the same kind
of thinking we used when we created them."

—ALBERT EINSTEIN

The summer of 1998 marked the splintering of Akamai's 50K team. There was no questioning the fact they had a great idea expressed in some beautiful theorems, but you can't sell theorems. Their business plan was flawed, their technology unproven and to date, they had not one line of code. A few of the initial advisors to the company lost interest, some lost faith. Others simply couldn't stay in Cambridge and wait for something to happen. Preetish Nijhawan, who first inspired the idea of forming a company for the competition, parted ways for a plum job at McKinsey & Co. in his hometown of Houston, Texas. Of the core team, however, Lewin, Leighton, and Seelig held fast to the idea that Akamai could be realized. In an act of faith—one aimed at protecting themselves against potential competitors—Lewin and Leighton submitted a patent application for Akamai's technology. They knew they couldn't stop anyone else from finding a way to speed up the Internet, but hoped that by making the mind-bending math underlying the Akamai software proprietary, they could prevent competitors from offering a better solution than their own."[1] Despite going their separate ways for the summer, they decided they would each forge ahead on their own: Lewin in New Jersey, Seelig in California, and Leighton in Massachusetts. Sometime around Labor Day weekend, they agreed, they would regroup in Cambridge and make what they knew would be a difficult decision: abandon Akamai or go full steam ahead.

That summer, Leighton's day job in Cambridge was to supervise a group of a dozen undergraduate students on a research project sponsored by LCS called Hacker Haven.* Leighton was given free rein with the students, so he decided to enlist them to try building a prototype of the Akamai technology. If it worked, Akamai would be able to prove the technology could function—at least in the confines of LCS. To motivate the young, industrious hackers, Leighton had what he considered to be a powerful force of inspiration: *Star Trek*. During the course of the 50K competition, the Akamai team connected with some representatives from Paramount Digital Entertainment, which owned the rights to the original *Star Trek* TV shows. With a plan in the works to eventually distribute all the old shows online, Paramount took great interest in Akamai's proposed technology. To demonstrate their enthusiasm, company executives sent a gigantic box filled with *Star Trek* paraphernalia to Leighton's office at LCS. He wisely used it as bait: "I passed out all these goodies and said, 'Look, if you guys build a prototype that actually works, we'll be able to distribute *Star Trek* TV shows.'" The result? "They went nuts. They worked around the clock."

Seelig spent the summer in the San Francisco Bay area, working at a consulting firm as a paid intern on a project for a Cambridge-based company called Cascade. With a few months to form West Coast connections that would be critical to Akamai's success, Seelig began meeting with everyone he knew and everyone in their collective Rolodexes. Friends. Family. Friends of family. And friends of friends. Gorenberg, the 50K judge at Hummer Winblad in San Francisco, was impressed enough by Akamai after the contest that he agreed to orchestrate some key meetings, most importantly with a worldwide data center company, Global Center, which Seelig would approach as a potential host for Akamai's servers. Through

---

*Here, the term "hackers" refers to a community of computer programming and systems design enthusiasts that originated out of MIT in the 1960s. This definition exists separately from today's mainstream usage of the word "hacker" to refer to cybercriminals.

investors at Sequoia Capital, Seelig was able to connect with someone at Yahoo, who offered hope of an eventual meeting with the company's founder, David Filo. Seelig also sought advice on a business model, which remained undecided. Marco Greenberg also came through with some big name connections, including a few potential investors in the world of media and entertainment.

At Bell Labs, Lewin enjoyed a more relaxed, predictable pace compared with the frenetic energy of his first few semesters at MIT. Built in the 1920s by AT&T, the lab's campus in Murray Hill, New Jersey, (later razed in 2002) was rich with prodigious intellect. The internationally renowned lab was the birthplace of some of the most innovative scientific advances of the century—radar, satellites, and the wireless network. In his book *The Idea Factory*, author Jon Gertner describes the atmosphere of the labs as both magical and eccentric. Scientists would crisscross the campus on unicycles and occasionally set off explosions.[2]

Despite the fact that he was tasked with several research projects for the algorithms group, Lewin spent a lot of the summer having fun. He shared a dorm at University of New Brunswick with three friends from LCS, including Yevgeniy Dodis and Anna Lysyanskaya. Together with a select group of students from all over the world, they caught a shuttle bus every morning for the one-hour drive to Berkeley Heights. In the spare time he had—evenings, or weekends when he didn't travel back to Cambridge—Lewin hung out with his roommates playing tennis, hiking, and canoeing down the Delaware River. "That summer, it was an incredible time," recalled Dodis. "There were so many of us there from MIT, and it was one of the happiest times of my life."

Even outside of MIT's earnest atmosphere, Lewin and his roommates didn't party. Every once and a while they'd enjoy a few beers, but most of their entertainment came from late nights challenging each other with math puzzles. In one e-mail, dated July 21, 1998,

Lewin sent a joking reply to fellow interns when it was suggested that he was slacking off.

FROM: Lewin Daniel <danl@research.bell-labs.com>

I object to your insinuation that people do work here. If you are trying to subtly suggest that we are not trying to get work done, then I can save you the perturbation: WE ARE NOT TRYING TO GET WORK DONE!
    —Danny

In fact, Lewin *was* working hard, focusing his research on problems related to Akamai. At the end of the summer, all interns at Bell Labs were required to present their work to the fellows and researchers. According to Dodis, these talks didn't usually draw a big audience, but the day Lewin presented, people packed into the large room to hear about his work to speed up the Internet. "When we walked in, he was already the center of attention. People were bombarding him with questions, but he was very confident. In that moment I saw him as this super ambitious guy," recalled Dodis.

By summer's end, Leighton had a promising development for Akamai from LCS. The prototype constructed by his Hacker Haven students was a success. To simulate a global network of servers, the students used separate floors of the Tech Square building: Paris was the seventh floor, and London sat on the sixth. They spent most of the summer cranking out the code to program the servers. With a batch of machines in place, they set up the mock network and created a functioning prototype. The biggest victory was demonstrating, inside the walls of LCS, the system's fault-tolerance: if they shut down one machine, the system would rebalance the data load and avert a crash. As the students increased the flow of traffic on the prototype, they were stunned to see it continued to run smoothly and efficiently. The more content they loaded into it, the better it performed, even under peak load.

The remaining critical question before Lewin, Leighton, and Seelig was their business model. How would they deliver this service? What would they charge? Even by midsummer, it was clear that no Internet Service Providers were willing to take a chance on Akamai. If they wanted to make the company work, they had only one choice: build the technology themselves. "We ran out of options," explained Leighton. But a clear business plan was still eluding them. For help, they turned to Todd Dagres, a shrewd, Boston-based venture capitalist at Battery Ventures.

Dagres had been introduced to Akamai before the 50K by a colleague at Battery, Scott Tobin, when the company was still Cachet, and Lewin, Leighton, Seelig, and Nijhawan were seeking out the support of investors. Initially, Dagres admitted he wasn't that impressed. "I remember thinking that they didn't really look like much," said Dagres. "Tom was nice and older and scholarly, and Danny—well, he did not look at all like a genius. He looked like a big kid, stocky but not overly imposing. They were academics and kind of nerdy." But the more Dagres got to know them, the more he grew to respect them. "These guys were very smart and if they didn't know something they would find someone who did," he concluded. What Dagres knew well, with his eyes on the trends in the high-tech sector, was how to take a great idea and turn it into a living, breathing business.

Favoring designer denim over finely tailored suits, and with a closely shaved head and athletic physique, Dagres looked more like a rock star than a financier. At Montgomery Securities and Solomon Smith Barney, Dagres had made millions as a technology analyst covering communications and the Internet, still in its infancy, later taking a job with Battery Ventures in 1994. Over time, he began to convince Lewin, Leighton, and Seelig that building and selling software wasn't going to work. Instead, Dagres was convinced they should offer a service on their own. "I thought they had something special and something they could use to build a recurring business," said Dagres. To him, the company's real powerhouse could be found in its algorithms—they were proprietary and so sophisticated they would be almost impossible for any competitor to replicate. "Instead of giving other guys the software or Akamai's 'secret sauce' and letting them skim the cream off the market, I thought Akamai should be the cream by building an annuity business with a big margin on this unique software," Dagres explained.

This made perfect sense, but it was a daunting proposition. It required capital, and lots of it, to build out a global infrastructure and buy and program all the servers. Installing Akamai servers in data centers around the world would cost hundreds of millions. But the most daunting aspect of the service model was not the cost; it was the customer expectations. To service these Web content companies, Akamai would have to provide service 24/7, 365 days a year. And it would have to do so with nearly 100 percent reliability.

Labor Day came quickly. And before they knew it, Leighton, Lewin, and Seelig were back at LCS with the decision before them. They each brought with them good news. Leighton had a functioning prototype. Lewin had fine-tuned the business plan. And Seelig had secured the support—both tentative and firm—of potential partners including data centers, content providers and hosting companies. "I spent a lot of time asking: 'If we can prove to you that your site will not crash and people all over the world will have a better experience, then would you be a customer?'" Seelig recalled. "In a sense we had to promise stuff that wasn't quite there yet—we were selling a vision and the challenge was that we needed both constituents—the content providers and the data centers—to nibble to make it work. It was like tap dancing."

The decision to go forward did not come easily. As Seelig put it, "I remember feeling like we'd proven enough that we could succeed; we vetted the technology and the market and had what I thought was a real prospect for success. But at the same time, I had no illusions that a prototype on the fifth floor of MIT's lab for computer science would guarantee it."

Then there was the competition already beginning to creep into the market. While no one was doing exactly what Akamai proposed, a handful of companies were pushing services that were similar enough to pose a threat. One of them was Adero, Inc., formed by David Crosbie, Akamai's ill-fated presenter at the 50K. Adero's business plan, which offered "infrastructure services" to content providers, was disconcertingly similar to Akamai's.

Logistically, the decision to start the business was easiest for Seelig; he could move back to his Cambridge apartment whereupon his parents would loan him some funds as a stopgap until Akamai could pay him a salary. For Lewin, however, the decision was weighty. For as much as he believed in Akamai, he also knew he had a lot to lose if it didn't succeed. He would have to continue taking at least one course to remain in MIT housing with Anne and the boys, but he'd lose his stipend, his only earnings. He'd also have to put his PhD candidacy on hold. Leighton knew that could be a perilous move for a student like Lewin, who was on the fast track towards a professorship. "He had a lot of doubts," said Leighton. "Once he committed to something he would plow forward, but this was not an obvious decision, and he agonized over it." It wasn't a totally effortless choice for Leighton, either. He was content where he was, with a steady income and job. But he had never taken a sabbatical. So maybe, he thought, it was time to take a chance.

In September 1998, Lewin and Leighton moved out of their offices at MIT and into a rented space at One Kendall Square, just down the block from LCS. Akamai Technologies was officially co-founded by Lewin and Leighton, Seelig and Randall Kaplan, the California businessman. Leighton still recalled an afternoon that fall when he and Lewin were walking from LCS to their new office at One Kendall. Lewin used the occasion for an impromptu pep talk, offering up all the reasons he believed Akamai would succeed. He told Leighton that it wasn't just their great technology, smart staff, or exemplary business plan that would guarantee success. "He said we had all those things, of course, but that wasn't why we were going to succeed," said Leighton. Instead, Lewin told him, "We're going to succeed because we're tenacious as hell."

Despite Lewin's bravado, he and Leighton felt some ambivalence. It didn't take rigorous math to understand that the odds were against them. According to the rule of venture capital, only one out of every sixty new businesses succeeds. "It was scary," recalled Leighton. "Danny was worried about it, and I was worried for him."

But in 1998, if you didn't move fast, you'd miss the moment. You'd be just another smart entrepreneur with a great idea left standing in the wake of the dot-com boom. Lewin charged forward at full speed.

CHAPTER 6

Kings of Cache

"We have an interface that makes you think,
'Click, and result,' so we want everything.
And we want it now."

— JAMES GLEICK,
Faster: The Acceleration of Just About Everything

On a winter day at the start of 1998, shocking news broke over the nation's front pages: President Clinton was accused of having an affair with a young woman in her twenties, Monica Lewinsky, a Pentagon employee and former White House intern.

With its salacious mix of power, sex, and political intrigue, the story gripped the media and the country, gathering steam when Independent Counsel Kenneth Starr (formerly assigned to the Whitewater investigation) took over the case. As the lurid details emerged, the public clamored for more.

On September 11, 1998, Congress conceded, releasing a 445-page report on the affair by the Independent Counsel Kenneth W. Starr. To release the entirety of the report (often called *The Starr Report*), law makers decided to use the Internet. It was the first time a widely read government document debuted online, and getting it there wasn't easy. Staffers at the House Oversight Committee had to take all the content of the report off the floppy disks it was saved on and transfer it all into Web files. When they were finished, they copied the Web files onto hundreds of CD-ROMs and delivered them to news organizations and government Web sites, leaving them to decide how best to manage the load. The media predicted the online release would cause a massive, nationwide meltdown of the Web. There was no meltdown, exactly. But when hundreds of thousands of readers eager for salacious details about the president tried to access the report, most of the government servers and news sites they logged onto froze or crashed completely. Even before the *Washington Post* actually posted the report, its Web site crashed as traffic soared to three times its load compared to

August 17, its busiest day, when Clinton testified before the start of the grand jury.[1]

It was a record-breaking day for the Internet, and, in some ways, defined the new medium the way the JFK–Nixon debates defined television. CNN.com recorded a historic three hundred thousand hits a minute, and MSNBC witnessed a one-day record with two million hits the first day it posted the report.[2] But it also brought one of the Internet's biggest weaknesses squarely into focus as dozens of major Web sites buckled under the traffic—and Akamai was uniquely poised to fix it.

One of Akamai's first checks came from Seelig's parents, Michael and Julie, for the sum of $50,000. The money went fast with rent to pay, staff to hire, and a system to begin building. It disappeared so fast that they scrimped and borrowed and began the relentless push to secure significant funding. Seelig wasn't too concerned; he had enough savings and family support to wait it out. Kaplan was in a similar situation, having come to Akamai from a lucrative position at SunAmerica. Leighton needed a salary, but he, too, had a safety net—a savings account, his wife's salary, and the option of returning to MIT if Akamai failed. In contrast, Lewin was broke. And with no guarantee of a profit in the near future, financial fears continued to needle him.

In October of 1998, Lewin drove to New York to attend the wedding of Greenberg to actress Stacey Nelkin, who was already pregnant with the couple's first child. Greenberg has never forgotten the eve of the ceremony, when Lewin showed up on the doorstep of his apartment, elated that he'd made it in time. Greenberg and Nelkin remembered Lewin having no qualms about asking to crash on the floor; he didn't have much of a choice. With no credit card and no funds for a night in a hotel, he seemed content to just curl up inconspicuously in a corner. Greenberg suggested that Lewin take a room in a new apartment the couple planned to move into, even though it was unfurnished, and handed him the keys. When Greenberg asked if Lewin wanted a blanket or something to sleep on instead of the bare hardwood floor, Lewin hesitated and said: "I guess I'll take a pillow." And off he went. The next day, Lewin held up the *chuppah* at the wedding for his best friend, then drove back to Cambridge.

At some point upon his return, Leighton helped Lewin work out a loan from Akamai's coffers to cover some of his expenses and keep him and Anne from falling into deep debt. Lewin knew that Akamai needed at least one or two of the investors who'd been flirting with the company to come through.

One of them was Arthur "Art" Bilger, a Los Angeles-based businessman who had just left a successful career in media as president and COO of New World Communications Group to invest in early stage companies. Bilger, who first heard about Akamai from Kaplan at a board meeting for an L.A.-based charitable organization, wasn't the most likely candidate for an angel investor. He didn't understand the math that formed the company's foundation, and he wasn't technologically savvy; he didn't even own a personal computer. But he liked Cambridge and was intrigued enough by what he heard from Kaplan to arrange to meet the team at MIT.

Over lunch, Lewin eagerly described Akamai to Bilger, a soft-spoken, bespectacled man. "I didn't know what the hell they were talking about," admitted Bilger. "But from the first meeting with them, one of my motivations was that, even in the worst case of it not working out, I'd learn a lot." Eager to learn more, Bilger returned to the West Coast and did some research, followed by a few trips to Cambridge to check on Akamai's progress. Bilger formed a close relationship with the small team. Over a short period of time, he became convinced Akamai would succeed. "In that moment, I decided to take their word for it," Bilger said. He knew they needed help with a first round of financing, so Bilger committed to investing in return for a personal stake in the company.

Around the same time, Akamai was fortunate to secure a meeting with Gilbert Friesen. A close family friend of Marco Greenberg, Friesen was a legend in the movie and music businesses. A gregarious charmer, he worked his way up from the mailroom of Capitol Records to found A&M Records with Herb Alpert and Jerry Moss. Friesen was responsible for the careers of music greats like Sting and hit films including the 1985 cult classic *The Breakfast Club*. Friesen grew A&M from a small operation out of a home garage to the largest indie label in the country. Greenberg had mentioned Akamai to Friesen, who made a career out of investing in early talent. Friesen was intrigued enough to meet with Seelig several times during his summer in CA and to introduce Akamai to some key contacts. Suddenly, Friesen said he began to think more about Akamai in late 1998: "The Internet technology drumbeat became intense; it was clearly a rare moment of tectonic change." Friesen added, "I just loved the name— Akamai. It was extremely sexy and different—a damn good name." Friesen had lunch with Randall Kaplan, who enthusiastically pitched Akamai, telling him he had so much faith in the company that he was investing $100,000 of his own money (in addition, he said he had convinced both his parents to invest). Friesen liked what he heard. He later picked up the phone, called Greenberg and asked, "When can I meet the guys at MIT?" A date was set, and sometime in September, Friesen—who knew so little about Akamai's technology he often mistakenly referred to it as "logarithms" instead of "algorithms"—flew to Cambridge to learn more. Despite the fact that he spent most of his time in the company of celebrities, Friesen found the academic atmosphere in Cambridge exhilarating. "I was out of my element, and it was exciting," related Friesen.

In that meeting with Akamai, Friesen became one of the first members of what had become a de facto fan club of Lewin and his performance in front of a whiteboard. In many ways, it was his canvas. With a pen in hand, he could stand in front of it for hours at a time and cover it with academic ideas—strings of (sometimes incomprehensible) math or business strategies. And when he did, his presentations could only be described as theatrical. The more he talked and scrawled, the more animated he became, hopping around and grinning from ear to ear as his ideas came to life on its smooth, white surface. As if on cue, he would intermittently turn and look out on his audience, gauging their interest and level of understanding. Friends liken Lewin's theatrics at the whiteboard to a freight train gathering steam until that stopping point when nearly everyone in the room sat silently wondering what, exactly, had just hit them. It was one of Lewin's most effective weapons.

Stunned by what he saw in Lewin at the whiteboard, Friesen said he felt a familiar sensation—the same one he experienced when he watched some of his top musical talents at the start of their careers. "Danny was like ambition and intellect on steroids," Friesen said. "His belief in this thing was so profoundly convincing that I believed, too." On the spot, Friesen pulled out his checkbook and handed them a check for half a million dollars. "I remember walking out of the building and thinking 'Friesen, what have you done?'" he said. "When people asked me what, exactly, does Akamai do, I'd say, 'I don't know.' But the thing I *did* know, when I made that commitment, was that Danny Lewin was a star."

Friesen became one of Akamai's key contacts on the West Coast and a willing point of contact for every potential investor or customer in his entertainment and media circles. He'd already connected Seelig with media companies and investors at Sequoia. In no time, he brought several more angel investors on board, including the publishing magnate Jann Wenner, Hard Rock Café co-founder Peter Morton, and the heavy-hitting New York attorney Joel S. Ehrenkranz.

With secured angel funds, Jonathan Seelig circled back to a company called Exodus Communications in San Francisco, California. Founded in 1994, Exodus had a massive global network of Internet data centers. Seelig had met with a team from Exodus several times over the summer, so he set up one more meeting with the company's president, Ellen Hancock. Lewin flew out to San Francisco so that he and Seelig could combine forces. They slept on the floor of a friend's apartment in the city and planned their pitch. Yet Exodus's services weren't cheap; it was the five-star data center complete with HVAC cooling systems, earthquake protection, a security system, and on-site power with multiple backup generators.[3] In the meeting with Hancock, Lewin presented Akamai's technology on the whiteboard. Hancock was so impressed she offered them a deal: Akamai could have space in almost a dozen Exodus service centers to install and unlimited connectivity for three months. If Akamai had raised startup funds by the end of the trial and was ready to launch, Exodus would begin charging for the space.

The injection of funds and the space to put servers allowed Akamai to begin the business in earnest: building the software, planning the deployment of servers with Akamai's technology, and finalizing agreements with a core group of beta testers. They also hired their first employees, including a handful of Leighton's Hacker Haven students, some other programming masterminds, and a network systems engineer named Bill Bogstad. By October, they were well on their way to launching Akamai's debut service, called FreeFlow. But to secure more money in a first official round of financing, they needed a business veteran. Or, as Todd Dagres of Battery Ventures put it, they needed a "risk mitigater." Akamai was still lacking in business gravitas; thus, in meetings with venture capitalists, their inexperience was often obvious. Seelig and Kaplan had some experience in the real world, but they were young. Lewin and Leighton were green. Before Battery Ventures would invest,

Dagres said, Akamai needed "an adult with business experience to help them run a service."

That adult was Paul Sagan. Sagan had recently moved with his family from Switzerland, where he enjoyed a prestigious, yearlong position as a senior advisor to the World Economic Forum. He came to Cambridge to find the next step in what had already been a wild ride in the news business. Born and raised on Chicago's South Side, Sagan's career in journalism began at the age of thirteen, when he earned $25 from a newspaper for a photograph he'd taken of a local car crash. He came by the profession naturally as the son of a newspaper publisher who'd always been interested in the way technology and new media shaped the news. With a degree from Northwestern University's Medill School of Journalism, Sagan joined WCBS-TV in New York where he began writing news at age twenty-two. "I was horribly underqualified," remembered Sagan, a bespectacled, tall businessman who is sharp-witted and affable. A serious, earnest young reporter, Sagan was the only staffer who dressed in a three-piece suit and tie at the office. He quietly but diligently worked his way up to a spot as the youngest news director in the history of the network.

After a decade at CBS, Sagan was recruited by Time Warner to start a news channel in New York called NY1, which he built from the ground up. He also helped to lead the company's online efforts with the launches of Roadrunner, the first cable modem service, and Pathfinder, one of the first Web sites in the world with advertising. In 1997, in his third and final job at Time Warner as president and editor of Time Inc. New Media, Sagan decided to make a change. By then, he had three children with his wife, Ann Burks Sagan, and he wanted to spend less time at the office and more with his family. When the stint at the World Economic Forum helping to plan the exclusive Davos conference came along, Sagan jumped on it. But after a year away from the hustle of a news-driven office, Sagan was ready for the next step. "I always loved the pressure of live TV news, especially the glory days when we did broadcasts at noon, five, six, eleven p.m.," he said. "And, at the time, a lot of people were saying the Internet was just as competitive and crazy." He began talks with some venture capitalists in the Boston area, starting with Battery Ventures, which he had connected with while working at Time Warner. Sagan was introduced to Dagres and Scott Tobin of Battery, who sent Sagan to "check out this crazy business plan" called Akamai.

Sagan did his due diligence. He read their crude business plan and Power Point presentation and met with Leighton, Lewin, and Seelig in Leighton's office at MIT, instantly taking a liking to the group. "They were super nice and super inquisitive," Sagan recalled. "I grew up in Hyde Park surrounded by University of Chicago academics"—his second cousin is the famous astronomer Carl Sagan—"so for me it felt like a natural fit."

Sagan took a clear message back to Dagres and Tobin: "I told them that I was no engineer, but that it looked to me like they had a working system. And if it works in the wilds of the Internet, they have a big idea worth investing in." Dagres trusted Sagan, but not everyone at Battery was convinced. "There were some doubts within my firm. One of my partners claimed that algorithms were not enough to build a company," noted Dagres. "But I really had faith in the people. I felt they knew something special and they'd work tirelessly to achieve a mission." To bolster his firm's confidence in Akamai, Dagres took an interesting proposition to Sagan: "We'll invest, if you'll go watch the money," he bargained. This because, as Dagres reasoned, "Sagan knew how to run a company, [and] he understood the media space and [was] smart and had high emotional intelligence." Sagan agreed to a six-month stint helping the theoretical mathematicians bolster their list of contacts, improving their business skills, and, of course, overseeing the money. He needed a title that would grant him the authority to make big decisions, so he took on the role of chief operating officer (COO). At that point,

Dagres said Battery had the confidence to invest in Akamai: "You never know for sure, but you take a shot."

With the belief that the big venture money was soon to come, Leighton signed the lease on a new office. Akamai moved from its tiny office space at One Kendall to the fourth floor of 201 Broadway in the heart of the Cambridge hub for high-tech firms. By November, everyone involved in the first-round financing rush was anxious—a deal was on the table, and it was a good one. Two prominent firms— Battery Ventures and Venrock*—were ready to make an investment of $8 million ($4 million each) in Akamai. The deal was as good as done, signed, and delivered to Akamai's financial officers and attorneys for vetting. But on a Sunday, the night before the funds were to be wired into Akamai's account, Leighton's home phone rang. It was one of the general managers of Venrock. "We're sorry," he told Leighton. "We're not going to close the deal." Leighton was stunned. Venrock seemed like the perfect fit, having been an early investor in both Apple and Intel. The partner went on to explain: "I've thought hard about it, and I don't think you're going to be successful."

Leighton could only think of one thing to say in response: "I think you're wrong."

In one phone call, Akamai lost half of the $8 million they'd been promised. Lewin immediately feared a domino effect after Venrock's sudden departure. Having turned down offers from almost all the local venture capital companies, they worried no one would even consider stepping in if Battery backed out, too. Dagres reassured them, though, offering to close the deal if Battery could take charge of finding another investor to fill the hole left by Venrock. Akamai agreed. Their best hope was Polaris Venture Partners, which had recently recruited George Conrades, a veteran from IBM and BNN (Bolt, Baranek Newman) who had long governed the intersection of business

---

*Venrock, founded in 1969, is the Rockefeller family's venture fund with offices in Massachusetts, New York, and California.

and cutting-edge technology. Dagres contacted Polaris with a deal: if the firm would supply the $4 million Akamai needed, the company would offer Conrades a position on its board. A deal was struck, and in November 1998, just before the Thanksgiving holiday, Akamai secured its first round of financing from Battery and Polaris.

Leighton and Lewin retained control of the company with a stake of $8 million. Lewin took the title of chief technology officer, and Leighton became chief scientist. Seelig assumed the role of vice president for Strategy and Corporate Development. Kaplan became vice president for Business Development.

After the deal was signed, everyone went home to celebrate the holiday. As for Venrock's last-minute decision, the true cause leaked later: the deal fell through not because Venrock lost faith in Akamai, but because a senior partner in the firm's New York office had butted heads with Lewin. "He thought Danny was arrogant and didn't like his demeanor," said Dagres. Venrock's decision to pass on the deal proved costly: if the firm had taken a 10 percent stake in Akamai for $10 million, it would have been worth $2 billion less than a year later.[4] Dagres said it went down as "one of the dumbest venture moves in history."

A young analyst at Venrock, who had worked around the clock to set the deal and, in the process, came to admire Lewin, sent him a book the week after the breakup. It was the inspiring story of a business mogul. Under the cover flap, he inscribed a note to Lewin: "You're a titan!" Lewin seized on the word. Not because it was used to praise him, but because he loved the ring of it. Titan! A word with mythological Greek origins that had also come to describe anything with a massive, indomitable spirit—from one of Saturn's moons to sports heroes and business magnates. It was pithy and powerful. Lewin kept the book in his office, and from that day forward, the word "titan" became a part of Akamai's vernacular, and it was reserved for the select few who exceeded even the highest expectations.

CHAPTER 7

Science or Snake Oil?

"Science is magic that works."

—KURT VONNEGUT,
Cat's Cradle

Akamai had money in the bank—lots of money. Despite the fact that the company still existed only on paper and in a student-built prototype at MIT, it was flush with cash. But to build the actual infrastructure, one formed by thousands of servers around the world, they would have to spend the bulk of it. Akamai had the space to install the servers through their commitment from Exodus. The company still needed to buy the servers, however, and somehow install them in the Exodus centers, some of which were located in remote corners of the globe. At the same time, they needed to sign up some content providers to try the Akamai service once it was up and running. To make all this happen quickly, everyone at Akamai again turned to connections. Lewin, Leighton, Seelig, Kaplan, and Greenberg scrambled to set up more meetings with friends, even friends of friends. They combed the MIT alumni database. They asked their investors to make calls and open doors on their behalf. They hopped on planes to meet with almost any interested party who offered them a few minutes of time. The hustle paid off.

Through a contact at Exodus, they found a San Diego–based company, True Solutions, to make four hundred servers. At the time, servers were not cheap, costing upwards of $10,000 apiece. But True Solutions was a little-known company without much of a track record, so they promised to quickly construct the servers to Akamai's exact specifications at a bargain price. Each of the servers would run on an operating system called Linux and would be programmed with software driven by Akamai's proprietary algorithms. Within a few weeks, True Solutions had already churned out approximately three hundred servers, and began shipping them out to eleven Exodus data centers in nine locations. Of those nine, only one of them was outside the U.S. But to Akamai, one server in London was enough to call their network international. With the servers in hand they needed to get them securely into the data centers. Exodus employees installed as many as they could, but left the rest to Akamai.

On a bitter December day, Lewin and Seelig drove out to a data center in Waltham, twenty minutes outside of Cambridge, to install one of Akamai's first racks of servers. "We literally threw these boxes of servers into the back of my car," said Seelig. It was after 4:00 p.m. when Lewin and Seelig pulled into the parking lot of the massive center located on Winter Street at the heart of the Route 128 tech corridor. Almost as soon as they arrived and began unloading, Lewin realized he'd forgotten their tool kit. They considered turning back, but they anticipated a few hours of work, and it was getting darker and colder. At that point, they decided they had only one option: the spare tire repair kit in Seelig's Mazda. They grabbed it, hauled their boxes into the building, and hoped for the best. It took four hours for the two of them to manually screw the servers into the racks, and by the end their fingers were throbbing. From the parking lot, they called Akamai to confirm a signal. The servers had been successfully connected, so Seelig and Lewin triumphantly headed home.

On the way, they spotted an Italian restaurant by the side of the road and decided to celebrate with a meal and a bottle of wine. "We were really excited," recalled Seelig. "Neither of us had heard of the place, but it looked good and we were hungry." It turns out they had stumbled on La Campania, a top-rated, pricey establishment popular with the venture capital partners in the surrounding offices. Clad in grease-stained jeans and covered in bits of cardboard and Styrofoam from breaking down dozens of boxes, Lewin and Seelig were hardly dressed for the occasion. "Danny and I were filthy," noted Seelig. "So we were a little uncomfortable when we sat down and spotted a few of these VC guys we'd been talking to about Akamai." A few minutes later, however, they realized the opportunity at hand. "One of these guys came by and asked us how things were going," said Seelig. "And we were able to honestly say, 'Great, we actually just came from one of our data centers.'"

Picture the Internet as a system of highways, one designed for the high-speed travel of data, or packets, around the globe.

It's a system that worked well early on, when the Internet served only a small community of users. But as traffic and the size of files began to increase exponentially, it became clear that the architecture of the Internet—a network of networks with no central point of command—wasn't built to withstand it.

By the mid-1990s, its major throughways were often congested and chaotic. For home users of the Internet, it was commonplace to type an address into the Internet's browser and wait an average of twenty seconds while the dial-up connection chirped, only to arrive at a frozen screen and the message "The server is busy...Please try again later." That's because the average request for information over the Internet had to make approximately nineteen hops before reaching its final destination.

Originally based on a combination of many algorithms created by Lewin and Leighton, Akamai's debut service, called FreeFlow, was able to process real-time information on traffic conditions and use it to trick the Internet's routers into sending data requests to Akamai servers at the edges of the Internet, closer to the end users. FreeFlow did two things to speed up the delivery of content and make Web sites feel faster. First, it adjusted BGP—the protocol used to make routing decisions on the Internet—to work almost in real time to direct data requests around the hot spots or traffic jams. Second, it cached, or stored, files on the servers in its own vast network that were closest to users.

With FreeFlow, Akamai created its own private path across the public Internet. Built entirely on software, it was a virtual road, one that took advantage of the Internet's architecture without relying on it. This enabled Akamai to offer its customers a number of benefits, chiefly fault tolerance. If one of Akamai's servers went down, the others in the network automatically picked up its workload until its service was restored. Another benefit to Akamai was ease of installation. To "Akamaize" their Web site, content providers followed relatively simple, step-by-step instructions to launch the FreeFlow software, which tagged the content or pages to be served by Akamai with an Akamai Resource Locator (ARL), Akamai's version of a URL, or Web address.

The value of FreeFlow went beyond the speed and efficiency of content delivery. Another benefit was maintenance. Customers didn't have to install or maintain any hardware, a major draw for the engineers who would otherwise have to spend time, money, and energy on finding a good fix when their sites reached peak traffic. Akamai also offered what it called "Proof of Performance," the guarantee that if FreeFlow failed to deliver a customer's content at any time, or failed to deliver it faster than the customer's own servers, Akamai would issue a refund.

To minimize the chance of failures, Lewin and Leighton immediately put one of the company's first rules in place: the Akamai office could never be empty. In order to provide customer service twenty-four hours a day, seven days a week, Akamai needed someone in the building at all times to troubleshoot. For at least the first year of business, this meant either Leighton or Lewin had to be there, too. This work commitment wasn't always easy on their spouses, both of whom were carrying the bulk of the domestic and parenting duties. Sometimes Anne Lewin or Bonnie Berger would arrive at the office in search of Danny or Tom, hoping to get their undivided attention on family matters. In February 1999, for example, a very pregnant Berger showed up in Akamai's lobby in search of Leighton, who had been too caught up to return any calls that day. When someone who had volunteered to locate Leighton asked her what the message was, Berger said: "I'm in labor!" The couple just made it to the hospital in time, welcoming their daughter, Rachel, into the family.

The potential perils of Lewin or Leighton being away from the office for any more than a day or few hours, however, were significant. If they weren't around, the programmers who spent hours translating Akamai's algorithms into code, which they often pushed out of the system well after midnight, could make an error with far-reaching consequences. "The programmers were fast and talented, but they weren't crossing all their *t*'s and dotting their *i*'s," said Leighton. "There were always bugs in the code, which was the price we paid for the [programmers'] speed. Either Danny or I had to be here to check [the code], or it would all blow up, and we'd have to go in and fix it." At such an early stage, they couldn't afford for things to go wrong. They'd spent the summer and start of fall of 1999 securing a non-binding commitment from big-name companies to try FreeFlow when it launched. The deal they offered was no cost to the companies—by signing on they agreed to test the service on a small portion of their content, ideally an image as tiny as a few pixels and embedded deeply on their Web site. From its headquarters in Cambridge, Akamai would then simulate peak loads of traffic to the select image long enough to prove the value of FreeFlow.

With the help of venture capital contacts and media mogul Gil Friesen, Lewin, Leighton, Seelig, and Kaplan, who worked out of California, were able to convince an impressive roster of ten beta testers to sign on. They included CNN, Disney, Yahoo, Geocities, MGM, Paramount, Warner Brothers, Universal, and Playboy. None of them were testing any real content with Akamai; as stated above, most started with one trial image hidden deep within their Web sites. But they were still some of the biggest names on the Web, and Akamai needed to secure a commitment from them beyond the trial stage. As COO, Paul Sagan swore everyone at Akamai to secrecy—cautioning them not to reveal the names of those who were still deciding whether they trusted the technology and the company. In addition, Akamai needed to maximize its public relations buzz. They had only one shot to announce an inaugural commercial launch. In an e-mail to the company on March 2, 1999, Sagan wrote, "If in doubt about what to tell people outside of Akamai, say less, not more. And refer them to me. Keeping a veil of secrecy about ourselves remains crucial. We don't want to tip off our competitors too early."

Akamai had no room for error. If the head of engineering for any one of these FreeFlow customers happened to log onto their Web site at 3:00 a.m. and notice the Akamaized content frozen or failing to load, they could easily cut ties.

As it happened, the first major glitch in Akamai's fledgling network had nothing to do with code. Sometime in January of 1999, the servers started to fail. Not just in one place but in many data centers, and no one at Akamai knew why. They considered outsourcing the repairs to Exodus, but this would take time. Instead, Sagan said, they decided to go at it alone: "We had to do it ourselves; we had to basically try to repair the network before the whole thing got disconnected." One of their first stops was an Exodus location at Boeing Field in Seattle. It was close to midnight when

Lewin and Sagan arrived at the colossal data center, a windowless, bunker-like building filled with racks of servers stretching from one end to the other. Lying on the cold floor surrounded by a few tools and myriad electronic parts, they pulled out the servers to diagnose the problem. It didn't take long. Almost as soon as they pulled the devices apart, they began finding loose screws. "They pretty much all had the same sloppiness," said Sagan. "I don't know if Danny even knew what he was doing, but if he didn't, he pretended to." Lewin and Sagan worked through the night to painstakingly disassemble each server, tighten its insides, and reinstall it into the racks. They later learned that, in a rush to fill Akamai's order for four hundred servers, the small California-based company True Solutions had hired inexperienced high school interns to put them together. The company shipped off the shoddily assembled servers, and once they were placed in the data centers, which were kept at low temperatures to protect the equipment, the loose screws had wiggled free, separating the components and causing the machines to crash.

The job of fixing the ailing servers was tedious and time-consuming, but it was a necessity. By the end of January, the servers were securely in place and Akamai was ready for the official debut of FreeFlow.

As a final test of the network's strength before launching, Akamai's engineers ran a load of data approximately six times the size of the heaviest traffic the largest news Web sites were struggling with. It barely hiccupped.

Image might have been the last thing on the minds of everyone at Akamai as FreeFlow took off. They were academics, and their work wasn't at all well-suited to the slick, fast-talking arena of publicity. But in the dot-com craze, generating buzz was a necessary element of success. Buzz made business moguls out of college students and helped build the astronomical market valuations of companies with little more than a cool-sounding business plan on paper. Akamai needed to create the impression that everyone who was anyone on the Internet was using its service. For this, Akamai turned to Marco Greenberg. In addition to his work helping Lewin, Leighton, and Seelig get Akamai off the ground, Greenberg had spent over a year building his own business, NYPR (New York Public Relations). He'd already garnered some big clients in the worlds of media, technology, and government, and was eager to officially take on Akamai. Before he was formally hired, Greenberg was interviewed by advisor Todd Dagres of Battery, who was drawing as much talent as he could into the company. Greenberg didn't have to prepare much; he knew Akamai inside and out and possessed stellar experience, including a few years as a manager in the corporate practice of global PR giant Burson–Marsteller, running big accounts including the Government of Israel. To Dagres, it was clear that Greenberg was much more than Lewin's friend—he was the best man for the job. Greenberg would remain in New York to manage his firm but travel to and from Cambridge once or twice a week for meetings and press duties at Akamai.

For Greenberg, it was a thrill to publicize Akamai. At the time, the media were eagerly pouncing on Internet startups with compelling background stories, and Greenberg knew just how to spin Akamai's. "The story was that these MIT scientists had found a way to make the World Wide Wait a thing of the past," explained Greenberg. "It was the right place and the right time." Greenberg said he never even tried to understand the nuances of the technology like an employee of Akamai or a techie; that wasn't his job. "I understood it just enough—I knew they were setting up these servers in various locations and that they would provide a richer experience for Internet users. My goal was to express it in layman's terms so that your grandmother could understand it. And my grandmother could."

In the first official press release, issued by Greenberg on January 14, 1999, FreeFlow, which Greenberg had named, was touted as "the world's largest fault-tolerant network for distributing Web content."[1] Greenberg distributed it to every possible outlet, and it began getting traction almost immediately. The media strategy, he said, was to go for the "big stuff" right away, well before plans were in place for an Initial Public Offering (IPO), and to emphasize the company's MIT connection.

Because of his age, charisma, and background, Lewin was the most obvious candidate for good press, but he wasn't always keen to engage in publicity. Some say he shied away from the spotlight, but according to Greenberg, he was just busy and focused on the day-to-day grind of running the company. Leighton felt likewise; he was happy to speak with the press, but preferred not to. Because of this, Greenberg often put Sagan out front, particularly when the press involved television. Because of his career in journalism, Sagan had inbuilt media savvy. He understood the impact of good press, and he also understood how to generate it. Most importantly, he was skilled at translating what Akamai did into something that sounded simple and impressive to a mainstream audience. When a sound bite was needed, he could serve one up. Even so, the media often got the facts muddled. On January 15, Sagan appeared on CNN for an interview with senior correspondent Steve Young, a veteran technology reporter. Sagan spent two full minutes explaining Akamai, after which Young turned to him with a perplexed look and said: "Paul, I'm not sure I fully get the concept. Are you selling equipment? A service? Both?" Patiently, Sagan started over.

The fact was, Akamai hadn't sold anything yet. The FreeFlow trial was going smoothly, but the ten trial customers weren't ready to trust a small company out of MIT with the bulk of their Web content. Akamai's first order of business, beyond the publicity blitz, was the hiring of a sales force. By early February, the company had a small team in place, led by John Sconyers and Earl Galleher, who both came from DIGEX, a Maryland-based Web hosting giant. Both Sconyers and Galleher were first introduced to Lewin, Leighton, and Seelig in the fall of 1998. At DIGEX, they were living with the problems of flash crowds and slow Web traffic on a daily basis, losing droves of customers frustrated by the company's inability to keep their sites up when traffic spiked. Galleher, who had been president of the Web Site division of DIGEX, said he didn't understand the computer science behind Akamai, but he *did* understand their business model and believed in it from the first time Lewin presented it to him on a whiteboard at MIT. "Danny got into this zone when he was just laying it out on the board and you could just see it all come to life," Galleher recalled. "You just knew it was going to work how he described it." At the time, Galleher offered his support and later contributed $25,000 to Akamai's first round of financing. "Danny knew that, technologically, I'm dumb as a brick—he could do his hashing algorithm talk for two days, and I wouldn't be any further along," remarked Galleher. "But it didn't take a rocket scientist to understand the pain corporations felt when they suffered network outages, and I knew it well."

At age thirty-nine, Galleher became Akamai's vice president of sales. One of Galleher's first tasks was to help Akamai set a pricing plan. At the time, the content delivery network (CDN) business model was so new that there was no industry standard. Akamai had a rough plan in place, one that would charge customers around $800 per megabit of data delivered per second. Galleher insisted the price was far too low. "They were looking at it mathematically," said Galleher. "But I was looking at it in terms of what the market would bear." Galleher suggested more than doubling the price to what he believed was the magic number: $1,995 per megabit per second. "Everyone scoffed at me," recalled Galleher. "And I told them, 'You know what? I'll fuckin' prove to you that I can sell it at this price.'"

And he did. When the company finally landed a full-price contract with Discovery Channel, it came in at $1,995. From that moment on, Akamai had in place a straightforward, service-based revenue plan, charging clients an even $2,000 per megabit per second per month. The pricing was based on each client's peak usage, which meant if it reached 5 megabits per second at any time during one month, Akamai would receive $10,000 for that month.

Galleher was a colorful character, known for his candid but sometimes brash demeanor. Lewin liked his passion, and the fact that he could always be counted on for a dose of humor. One story in what became the "Legend of Galleher" involved a debate within Akamai over whether or not to work with Playboy Corp., based out of Chicago, as a customer. "We'd done some soul searching, and at first many people on the board [of directors] were against the idea of it because to them it meant we were carrying porn," said Dagres, who was involved in early talks with the company. "But we could also justify it with the fact that the U.S. Postal Service was Playboy's biggest distributor." Dagres recalled one meeting in particular when he asked the representatives from Playboy about their Internet service needs, and one of them mentioned their worries about site security. "Are you concerned someone might hack into [it] and put porn on it?" Dagres joked. The line fell flat. "I swear you could hear a pin drop," he said. It took a particularly rough quarter for sales, however, to iron out any internal conflict over Playboy. Dagres related that, during a board meeting focused on how Akamai would make its sales mark for the period, Galleher commanded the room. "I have a solution," he said. "Porn." Galleher said this in jest, but there was some truth in his words. Pornography companies were early adapters of Internet technology and arguably the first e-commerce businesses. And, because of market demand, they were willing to pay for top-tier content delivery. With this in mind, executives at Akamai agreed. The company agreed to limit the customer base in that sector to sites they deemed acceptable, which included Playboy. Still, the decision became fodder for company-wide jokes like the name "Naughty NOCC," referring to the Akamai's "Network Operations Control Center," where someone at the company was delegated to monitor the Playboy Web site.

John Sconyers, a graduate of MIT's Sloan School, had spent a few years managing all of the New England accounts for DIGEX. At age twenty-nine, he became Akamai's twenty-third full-time employee, joining the company a month before Galleher as senior account manager. Sconyers knew that, to gain momentum, Akamai would have to sign on at least two-dozen big names as customers—and do so quickly. But selling a service that few people fully understood wasn't going to be easy. Competitors like Sandpiper and Inktomi both offered caching and mirroring services that were intelligent enough to pose a threat and already had market traction. But the greatest threat, both Sconyers and Galleher knew, didn't come from the competition. It came from what they called "do-it-yourself" (DIY). This meant the companies so desperate for a way to manage escalating Web traffic that they were building their own solutions with huge amounts of money, massive infrastructure and highly skilled engineers. The idea of swooping in on a company like Yahoo, for example, and suggesting that Akamai's solution—one rooted in obscure theoretical math—was better than its own, risked sounding more like bravado than brilliance. "At that time, what we were doing was not obvious, and most people thought we were totally nuts," Sagan said. "It wasn't so much that we had skeptics. It was that we didn't really have believers."

To win over a critical mass of customers, Akamai's tiny sales force set out with almost evangelical zeal. They understood the virtuous circle, or network effect, of their business model—the more customers they won over, the higher performing Akamai's service would be because it would be handling more data, further proving its excellence. Galleher and Sconyers set out almost immediately, flying all over the country to meet with content providers, usually with a few recent MIT graduates in tow—newly minted engineers wearing baseball hats and backpacks. "I was out on the road and taking these brilliant kids with me," Sconyers recalled. "It was certainly the first business trip they'd ever been on, and there we were meeting with CTOs and other top executives of these media giants, who set the vision and controlled budgets of tens of millions. It wasn't as if we were going out to meet with a pizza joint or a plumbing shop. It was Disney, it was Yahoo, it was CNN, and it was Universal. And all of us were jumping on planes every week, flying around to get this all started. It was just thrilling."

When the meetings didn't go well, or there was an intractable technology expert to convert, Lewin, or one of Akamai's other executives, would deliver the pitch. It quickly became apparent that, when it came to sales, Lewin was the company's most powerful weapon, capable of turning skeptics into true believers. "A lot of meetings would begin with some decision maker saying, 'Thanks for coming to Seattle, but I've only got twenty minutes. My boss told me I had to take this meeting, so sit down and tell me what you have to say,'" Sconyers remembered. "Two hours later, Danny would still be at the whiteboard in full throttle, with a room full of technology staff in rapt attention." Galleher, who traveled thousands of miles with Lewin to make sales calls, recalled: "Danny was so focused on getting everyone in the room to experience this euphoric passion, one that made them believe 'I don't know exactly what this is, but I need to have this, and I need to have it now.' Once he got the customer to this frothy pitch level of excitement, he'd basically leave the room, and I'd close the deal."

Galleher added, "The fact was, these customers had a need, and they weren't aware that it was possible to solve it our way because nothing [else] like Akamai existed. The persona of Danny rapidly created a market perception that we were intensely smart and what we were doing was highly relevant."

While the sales team traversed the country in the early months of 1999, Akamai's staff in Cambridge, which was growing steadily, continued to build the network's infrastructure. At the time, they had no more than a few hundred servers, all but one set in the US. The more customers they signed, the more points of service they would need. There was also the threat posed by the competition. To beat them, they needed to be the first to install their servers in data centers. "That way, if anyone came on and said they wanted space to do what Akamai was doing, we'd already be there," reasoned Sagan. "We saw it as a land grab for beachfront property."

As VP of Strategy and Corporate Development, Seelig's focus was Akamai's infrastructure, a complex, highly sophisticated network of servers that remained in constant contact with each other, using their own unique language of Linux, a computer operating system. Seelig described the task of managing the installment of the servers—pre-programmed with Akamai's software—in data centers worldwide as a logistical nightmare. An international shipping company was in charge of delivering the servers, along with the cables, switches, and instructions, to their physical destinations. Once the servers were on location, Akamai's partners at the data centers installed them. Still, Akamai constantly experienced snafus related to shipping damages or extreme weather. In addition, as Akamai rapidly added servers around the world, its connection to servers in the most distant countries was sometimes so poor that Seelig said they had trouble confirming it.

As chief scientist, Tom Leighton worked mainly out of Cambridge during Akamai's first year. Occasionally, he traveled for sales calls or investor meetings, but the focus of his job was the technology—often referred to as Akamai's "secret sauce." As Leighton explained, "It was more of an inward role. I spent the bulk of my time improving our architecture." But with a small staff and a never-ending list of responsibilities, Leighton—like everyone at Akamai—had to do a little bit of everything. "For a while, I *was* our customer service department," said Leighton, who took many late-night calls when a connection unexplainably went down. "In those days, it was stressful because the service wasn't really [fully] 'baked,' and our description of it was often far grander than what it really was," admitted Leighton. "Every once in a while, I'd hear Danny promise something and think, 'Uh oh, now we've gotta deliver on that, and it was a challenge.'"

Akamai had a list of most wanted customers, and Disney was close to the top. But it was a tough culture to crack: a long established corporate giant with a Byzantine internal structure. Moreover, in 1998, Disney bought Starwave Corp./Infoseek, a Seattle-based software and Web company led by billionaire Paul Allen, who cofounded Microsoft. Starwave set the standard for much of the commercial Web explosion of the decade. Having recently merged with Infoseek, Starwave was developing major sites like ESPN.com and Mr.Showbiz.com. Disney's acquisition of the Starwave/Infoseek conglomerate formed a new giant, Walt Disney Internet Group. Randall Kaplan made one of the first connections to the company through Jake Weinbaum, then chairman of Disney's Internet Group.

Weinbaum directed him to contact Randy Dragon, an engineer who managed all the online operations for Disney Interactive Studios in Los Angeles. Disney hired Dragon from Columbia Pictures in 1985. But it wasn't until 1999 that the company started Disney.com under the leadership of Chairman Michael Eisner. Eisner's vision for his company's online presence was grand, and because of this he gave Dragon's fifteen-person staff a few years' free rein to build the site. As a corporate behemoth, Disney had first turned to top leaders in technology like ATT's Bell Labs to help the company find the ideal hosting service. "But the big guys didn't have a clue about infrastructure," Dragon noted. "And neither did we." With the desire to launch a Web site rich with media at a time of dial-up Internet connections, Disney was struggling. The acquisition of Starwave didn't help—the company had its own engineers running ESPN's blockbuster site, but Dragon didn't see long-term promise in their infrastructure either. Toward the end of 1998, Akamai showed up with a solution. Dragon recalled one of their first meetings: "With their white socks and buttoned-up look, they were a little strange to us—they were so academic," Dragon said. "But the idea they presented was so impressive, and it was clear they'd really thought it through. They weren't trying to put the hard sell on us, they were really trying to create a solution, and it was amazing."

Dragon agreed to sign Disney on as one of Akamai's first trial customers. Sometime in February 1999, Dragon called Akamai saying he felt the FreeFlow trial had gone really well, and that he wanted to sign up with Akamai, but needed to review the company's standard Service Level Agreement (SLA). John Sconyers in sales took the call, and agreed to send one along that day. He hung up and realized they didn't yet have any such agreement. He called on Leighton, who, with the help of several engineers and Akamai's General Counsel Robert Ball, spent two hours drafting language that would hold Akamai accountable to customers for superior performance. Akamai still wasn't generating any revenue, but they now had the promise of it. "We didn't really have any business yet," Leighton said. "We had one object deep on Disney's site where no one would go. We were hitting it every few minutes ourselves just to see if it was still there." Akamai needed to prove itself. The trial tests were running better than expected, but the company was still selling a vision; the promise of a service so powerful it could keep the most popular Web sites online during an unprecedented crush of traffic. For Akamai to fulfill that promise in real time, live on the Internet, they needed to test their software during a naturally occurring, high-traffic surge. As good luck would have it, two traffic surges happened soon thereafter. And by sheer coincidence, they took place on the very same day: March 11, 1999.

It was the first day of "March Madness," the annual NCAA basketball tournament. It's one of the most-watched sporting events of the year, one that attracts millions of fans who tune in every day for three weeks to watch their favorite teams duke it out for the championship title. By the mid-1990s, at least two companies were broadcasting the tournament live on the Internet: Infoseek (which hosted ESPN's Web site) and SportsLine USA. Both were experiencing historic amounts of traffic, with page hits exceeding 160,000 a minute.[2] Around lunchtime that day, someone from Infoseek called Akamai with two urgent questions: How could they sign up for FreeFlow? And could they do so immediately? Leighton was shocked. Akamai had been in aggressive pursuit of Infoseek, one of the most popular search engines on the Web, but had been rebuffed. Within fifteen minutes of the call, though, Akamai was delivering a portion of Infoseek's traffic. The phone rang again. It was another call from Infoseek, with another pressing request: Could Akamai handle a load of 2,000 objects per second? "We had no choice but to say 'Sure, we can do that,'" said Leighton. Within a few minutes, Akamai was successfully delivering three thousand objects per second for Infoseek. Leighton said they didn't know then that the company was hosting the NCAA tournament on ESPN's Web site, which had crashed almost as soon as the games began. With Akamai's help, Infoseek was back online and five times faster than they'd ever been before.

That night, Akamai was hosting a small gathering of investors for the screening of a trailer for the fourth, highly anticipated Star Wars film, *Episode I: The Phantom Menace*, which was premiering in theaters nationwide a week later. Earlier in the month, someone at Paramount's *Entertainment Tonight* show had contacted Akamai asking if the company could deliver the trailer for its Web site on the night of its release. An agreement was signed. Unbeknownst to anyone at Akamai, Star Wars producer and director George Lucas had struck a deal with Steve Jobs, interim CEO at Apple, for a blockbuster release of the trailer on Apple.com and Lucas's Starwars.com using Apple's new QuickTime III video player technology.[3] Around 9:00 p.m. that night, a room full of Akamai employees and investors tuned in to the live stream of the trailer on the FreeFlow-enabled Web site of *Entertainment Tonight*, which went off without a hitch.

Shortly after the screening, someone at Akamai burst in the room with breaking news: Apple's Web site had crashed! So had a handful of other Web sites as they attempted to stream bootlegged copies of the Star Wars trailer to more than twenty million viewers worldwide. The only sites that remained live, streaming the trailer without any outages or delays, were Paramount.com and *Entertainment Tonight*. Akamai's FreeFlow handled up to 3,000 hits per second for the two sites—250 million in total—and the system never exceeded even 1 percent of its capacity. In fact, as the download frenzy overwhelmed other sites, Akamai picked up the slack. Before long, Akamai became the exclusive distributor of all *Phantom Menace* QuickTimes, serving both Starwars.com and Apple.com.

It was another victory for Akamai, one so significant that news of it quickly made its way through the industry, allowing the company to approach more choice customers with greater credibility. The first of these names was a crazy-sounding business out of Stanford called Yahoo.

Yahoo burst onto the scene in 1994 when David Filo and Jerry Yang, both PhD candidates in Electrical Engineering at Stanford University, created an online list of their favorite Web sites. When the list grew so big it became unwieldy, they broke it down into categories, then subcategories. What started out as "Jerry and David's Guide to the World Wide Web," became Yahoo, one of the most popular search engines on the Web. In just a few months, Filo and Yang's pet project had reached a peak of one million hits a day. The pair incorporated in March of 1995 with an initial investment of $2 million from the California venture firm Sequoia Capital. By the time Akamai launched, Yahoo was a household name. In the dot-com boom, a working relationship with Yahoo held so much clout it could put an otherwise struggling startup firmly on the map. And Yahoo knew this. "The environment was such that any idea [for a dot-com startup] had four or five people [working on] it at the same time, all of them backed by big investors, and the first thing they'd say is, 'Go see AOL and Yahoo and get them,'" explained Farzod Nazem, an angel investor who served as Yahoo's first chief technology officer (CTO). "I say this with the ultimate humility: we were kingmakers."

But even for Akamai, a company built on the idea of scale, Yahoo was a hard sell for one main reason: it was growing so fast that no one could catch up. By necessity, Yahoo was mostly self-sufficient, even when it came to managing its peak congestion. "The scope of Yahoo was so large at the time that there was literally no vendor that could handle our traffic," said Nazem. "But we had a lot of small objects and a lot of traffic, and we needed to be able to serve these things without melting down." Using a combination of hardware and software as well as partnerships with peering points—two networks who agree to accept and forward each other's data packets—Yahoo was able to shoulder a heavy load. But the more Yahoo grew, the more urgent was its need to outsource.

At the time, you had to know someone who knew someone at Yahoo to get a foot in the door. Fortunately for Akamai, that someone was Michael Moritz at Sequoia Capital, who helped Akamai secure a meeting with founder David Filo in 1998, but nothing came out of it. Lewin, however, wouldn't take no for an answer. Sometime at the start of 1999, he and Sagan flew out to Yahoo's Santa Clara, California offices to meet with a group including Filo and Nazem. Nazem reckoned that he and Filo might have seen representatives from every significant startup of the decade come through their offices, and smart, driven entrepreneurs like Lewin led most of those startups. But Lewin, they agreed, made one of the few lasting impressions from the whirlwind year that was 1999. "We were impressed with Akamai in general, and I think a lot of that had to do with Danny," remembered Filo. "Most of the time, when you're dealing with someone trying to sell something, you're talking to a salesperson. But we were talking to Danny and the other founders, and they clearly had the strongest technical team out there." Nazem concurred, and they decided to strike a deal with Akamai.

Paul Sagan clearly recalled the moment Filo asked him and Lewin for the documentation he needed to become an official test customer. When they handed the stack of paperwork over to Filo, he took one look at it and asked if he had to complete it all to "Akama-ize." "Of course, we wanted to burst out loud cheering and kiss him," said Sagan. But we remained very poker-faced and mumbled something about how we could certainly work something out to waive some of the requirements." Sagan and Lewin assumed that, like most of their big-name customers, Filo would want to test the FreeFlow technology on one hidden pixel buried deep on Yahoo's site. Instead, Filo surprised them with a request to stream the Visa logo, which the company displayed on every one of its home pages. "We told him something like, 'OK, I suppose we can do that,'" Sagan said.

Sagan and Lewin told Filo they'd have someone at Akamai immediately send over a content code he could use to retag the Visa logo. When he'd done this, Filo just needed to email it back to Akamai's offices in Cambridge, and they'd immediately start serving the image. On the way out of the building, Lewin called the student who was in charge of the programming team that day. "He told him, 'You're going to get a message from David Filo—the *real* David Filo—so you need to make sure you don't fuck this up!'" Within minutes, they got a return call from the student saying that Filo had successfully Akamaized the logo. Yahoo was officially a client. Lewin called Leighton with the news. "It was mind-blowing for us," declared Leighton. "At the time, Yahoo was the who's who of the Internet, and suddenly we were [delivering a portion of content] on their homepage."

Sagan and Lewin left Yahoo's offices in their rental car, which had, by chance, been upgraded to a Mustang convertible. On their way up Highway 101, they opened the roof and shouted at the top of their lungs: "Ya-hooooooooooo!"

If anything had the potential to demonstrate the limitations of the Internet under stress, it was breaking news. "Some of the largest and most unpredictable hot spots were in the news business," said Sagan, who experienced the problem firsthand when he served as president of New Media at Time, Inc. And when news sites crashed, the cost to the organization was immeasurable. "Reputations in news could be made or broken on the day of a big story," Sagan said, noting that a banner day of breaking news coverage could result in a ten-year run of dominance. The same was soon true, he explained, of news online: "It became essential to win stories on the Web." Akamai was perfectly poised to help news organizations that wanted to win more online followers. The biggest and most popular of these was CNN.com.

At the end of August 1995, CNN Interactive launched CNN. com. It rapidly became one of the busiest sites on the web, and within two years had expanded to include CNNFN (Financial Network), and CNNSI (Sports Illustrated). Sam Gassel, then the chief systems engineer for CNN Internet Technologies, had served as the architect of CNN's web system since its launch. Even before joining CNN he had been building web servers as a systems administrator for the University of Chicago.

One of Gassel's greatest challenges was managing the flash crowds generated by breaking news, which he and his team of experienced engineers were working diligently to tackle. When traffic peaked, they turned to a large arsenal of technological weapons and strategies including the reallocation of a server from one of CNN's less trafficked Web sites to one struggling or stripping content down to the bare minimum by removing photographs and logos that occupied bandwidth. As early as 1997 they had also begun to experiment with caching technologies.

Gassel first met with Jonathan Seelig and John Sconyers in the fall of 1998. Recognizing the Akamai concept as a logical step forward, he was intrigued, but skeptical. "I told them if you can build this and run it—and we have our doubts—then get back to us." The dialogue continued and after a few more calls with Sconyers, Seelig and Lewin, Gassel agreed to test an invisible image on one of CNN's sites as part of Akamai's test trial.

A few months later, Lewin and Sagan took a trip to Atlanta determined to score CNN as a customer. Lewin was armed with what he believed to be a compelling point in his sales pitch: CNN could one day see a news event so huge that no amount of servers or bandwidth could handle it. The Internet users of the world would turn to CNN, which billed itself "the most trusted name in news," only to find blank or skeletal Web pages.

Gassel clearly recalls his first encounter with Lewin: "He was a bundle of energy," he said. "And he was awestruck when he saw both the newsroom and all our racks of servers." Sagan, who knew Gassel from when he [Sagan] had worked at Time Inc.'s Pathfinder likened that first face-to-face conversation between Lewin and Gassel to an intellectual ping-pong match, with each of them lobbing high-level concepts at the other.

Gassel also recalls a later visit that was interrupted by breaking news. Watching and listening to the CNN engineers methodically reconfiguring their systems to redirect traffic and avert a crash, Lewin remarked: "You guys sound exactly like Israeli tank commanders!" Gassel added: "He reassured me that this was a compliment."

Other news organizations followed, including *The Washington Post*. For years, Eric Schvimmer, director of operations for the newspaper's Web site, had been trying to combat flash crowds using every possible method. But he and his staff were failing, Schvimmer said, when it came to huge news events like the 1996 presidential election. By 1999, though, Schvimmer admitted, the problem "was keeping me up at night." "We were scaling more and more hardware, but we just couldn't keep up on the server side." Schvimmer had met with Lewin and Leighton a few months earlier and was impressed with what they proposed. But he also remained skeptical. Once he heard Akamai was serving traffic for CNN, however, Schvimmer petitioned the *Post* to invest in a service agreement with Akamai. "It was a no-brainer to me," he said. "We had this opportunity to get the very same service that the big boys had." By February 1999, the newspaper was testing content with Akamai, and its Web site was functioning better than Schvimmer could have ever imagined.

There's good publicity and bad publicity. And then there's the kind of publicity no amount of money can buy. In the late 1990s, a glowing feature on an up-and-coming company posted on The Motley Fool's Web site could send Wall Street into a state of frenzy. Founded in 1993 by brothers David and Tom Gardner,

Motley Fool's free Web site, Fool.com, had grown from a readership of just sixty into one of the most consulted online financial forums, one popular for its candid, humorous, and skeptical financial news and advice. (The company took its name from an Elizabethan drama, where only the court jester, or fool, could tell the king the truth without getting his head lopped off.)

The chief technologist at The Motley Fool was a graduate student at Georgetown University, Dwight Gibbs. Gibbs began messing around with computers in the fifth grade and learned to program and write software. In September of 1994, while working toward an MBA, Gibbs was hired to help Fool.com. In his role as "Chief Techie Geek," Gibbs explained that he was charged with "pretty much anything and everything," including database design, user support, and programming. By 1998, the site was nearing one million visitors per month, and it was crashing—a lot. Gibbs's quest, as he recalled, was not to find the best hosting provider. It was to find the one that "sucked the least." The courtships were fast and ended furiously. The Motley Fool moved its Web site six times in seven years. By the fall of 1998, the site was flooded by peak traffic of more than ten million users, and it buckled under the pressure. Gibbs noted that the last, and by far the worst, hosting provider was DIGEX, where Earl Galleher was formerly president of the Web division. Gibbs was losing faith that the Motley Fool could find a solution, and he was getting assailed with posts on the site's message board like "Your site sucks." The Motley Fool ended its contract with DIGEX three months early.

A few months after Fool.com severed ties with DIGEX, Earl Galleher, who had left the company for Akamai, called Gibbs at home and asked for a meeting. "We want to know what went wrong," he said. Gibbs met Galleher and a few others and "let them have it." Galleher didn't flinch—he listened and left. Several months later, Gibbs got another call from Galleher. "I have an answer to your problems," he said. To Gibbs and his team, Akamai's technology sounded more like snake oil than a practical solution. To them, the idea that a bunch of MIT guys had an answer out of their ivory tower was nothing short of preposterous. "A couple of geeks at MIT are going to fix the Internet," Gibbs remembered thinking. "How cute." But Galleher had taken the time to listen to Gibbs, and now, Gibbs agreed to return the favor and meet with one emissary from Akamai.

On an inferno-like day in Washington, DC in late August of 1998, Lewin flew into Reagan Airport and took a taxi to the Motley Fool headquarters in Alexandria, Virginia. Gibbs was still shrugging off the meeting. His tech team, he recalled, was ready to rip into Lewin, the nerd from MIT, for his audacity. Gibbs kept Lewin waiting for close to fifteen minutes before heading to the lobby to meet him. Lewin was unfazed. And Gibbs was surprised by Lewin from the moment he met him. Lewin practically bounced off the couch and darted over to Gibbs to shake his hand—"I'm Danny," he said, disarming Gibbs from then on. Lewin was nothing like the PhD scientist Gibbs expected; he was friendly, animated and full of pep. Gibbs ushered Lewin to the basement floor of the building, an unfinished room with no ventilation that served as a makeshift conference area. Lewin's audience, a ticked-off tech team of over twenty guys, was lying in wait like a bunch of hungry seagulls. The heat made things worse. Lounging disrespectfully in their chairs, they waited for Lewin to start his show.

Lewin turned to the whiteboard and began. An hour into the presentation, Gibbs remembered a palpable shift in the room. His guys moved forward in their chairs, training their eyes squarely on Lewin as he grew more engaging. Another hour passed; by this time, Lewin had covered the whiteboard and, without hesitation, began to write on the unfinished wall. When he stopped, they began firing questions at Lewin. Lewin fired right back. Not even the smartest of

Gibbs's tech guys could poke holes in Lewin's ideas. More than three hours later, Lewin packed up and left. Gibbs reported a collective feeling of awe. My guys looked at me and said, "He's scary smart, and this might actually work."

Still, the question of whether to go with Akamai was fraught with skepticism. Lewin had wooed them with his intellect and magic at the whiteboard, but would the technology really hold up? They spent two weeks deliberating. Meanwhile, The Fool was getting crushed with traffic, and they needed a solution—fast. They couldn't keep buying servers or spending days on end in the office at the ready when one crashed.

By early 1999, The Motley Fool entered into a contract with Akamai, first on a trial basis and then, once the company ironed out a few glitches, as paying customers. Gibbs became one of Akamai's most ardent advocates, often posting comments on The Fool's message boards singing its praises, always with the candid disclaimer that he was a customer.

There was plenty to cheer about; customers were still calling on Akamai. One of the first during that feverish spring sales period was Sean Moriarity, then-president and COO of Ticketmaster. At the time, event ticketing was still largely an offline business, but Moriarity, a self-taught technologist, saw the potential in e-ticketing. One of the greatest barriers to growing the business, however, was how to handle the flash crowds that would swamp Ticketmaster's site the very minute tickets to a popular event went on sale. At some point, Moriarity said he read about Akamai and was intrigued (and frustrated) enough to contact the company and request a meeting, which took place in June 1999 in Pasadena, California. "Engineers are skeptical by nature, and the ones I worked with were no different," Moriarity said. "But Danny came along and operated at such a high level that you could feel the skepticism in the room just melt away." After investing massive amounts of resources into Ticketmaster's Web operations, the company had a solution in FreeFlow. Moriarity recalled: "When I look back I think a lot of my belief in Akamai came from Danny's vitality. Most people who are that intelligent are defined by their intelligence, but he was defined by his passion; it was infectious."

The next call was from Apple. At the time, the company based in Cupertino, California didn't have a lot of content on the Web. But, as a pioneer in the personal computer business with Steve Jobs at its helm, Apple had grand plans to expand vastly into several segments of Internet-based technology. Of these, streaming audio and visual media were two priorities that Apple was struggling with. Akamai had been pursuing Apple for some time, with the knowledge that the opportunity to enter into any partnership with the company would mean instant credibility and an unrivaled cool factor. At some point, Lewin and a few others from Akamai met with Eddie Cue, who was creating Apple's first online store, and Frank Cassanova, director of marketing for the company's new multimedia site, QuickTime TV. Lewin delivered a passionate pitch to them on the whiteboard promising a partnership between Akamai and Apple that would revolutionize television. They thanked everyone and left. But nothing came of it.

Regardless, the contracts from paying customers were beginning to arrive, and at 10:00 p.m. on the night of March 31, 1999, the office received a momentous fax from Randy Dragon at Disney Online in Burbank. It was Akamai's first long-term service order for the billing period beginning April 1st, with a monthly commitment of $4,760. John Sconyers framed it, and hung it proudly on the wall of his office. About the same time, the official service agreement from Yahoo arrived. David Filo and Farzod Nazem had signed it and sent it to Akamai along with a one-dollar bill, on which Nazem wrote

"Good Luck." Sagan framed it and hung it in his office. Akamai had received its first dollar.

The next day, on April 1, 1999, Sagan arrived to work early to meet with advisory board member Art Bilger. Just as he sat down at his desk, the phone rang. Sagan answered, and the voice on the other end said, "Hi, this is Steve Jobs, and I want to buy your company."

For a second, Sagan was speechless. His first thought was that the caller was his brother, Alex, playing a prank on him for April Fool's Day. "I almost said, 'Fuck you, Alex,' and hung up the phone," said Sagan. Instead, he replied, "Steve, nice to meet you. Our company is not for sale, but we'd love to be partners." The call began three months of tough negotiations with Jobs, who initially offered up $16 million in cash to purchase Akamai. Because Akamai really wasn't for sale, Jobs began pushing aggressively for a strategic partnership.

In its first month of commercial service, Akamai's FreeFlow delivered more than ten billion hits for some of the biggest players on the Internet. The company's fax machine was busy receiving customer invoices and service agreements, and Steve Jobs had come a courting. Akamai was officially on the map.

CHAPTER 8

The Go-Go Days

"It's hard to tell with these Internet startups
if they're really interested in building companies
or if they're just interested in the money. I can
tell you, though: If they don't really want to
build a company, they won't luck into it.
That's because it's so hard that if you don't
have a passion, you'll give up."

—STEVE JOBS

Everyone at Akamai knew that if they had one shot in life, they were looking right at it. If they stayed in the game, kept up the pace and trounced the competition, they could become the next dot-com dream. And they could become rich—absurdly rich. The speculative bubble was still on the rise, fueled by a steady influx of Internet IPOs with no revenue or profits and market values in the millions. Amazon.com, the Internet bookseller, had not reported a profitable quarter since its IPO in May 1997, but in the first week of trading in the new year, its share price soared by nearly fifty percent.[1]

On Wall Street, common sense had given way to irrational exuberance. In the first four months of 1999, the Dow Jones Internet Composite Index doubled. Dot-com stocks offered the fastest road to prosperity, and in their zeal to capitalize on them, investors took the typical three-year trajectory from business plan to incorporation and cut it as short as the markets would allow. In *Dot.Con: How America Lost Its Mind and Money in the Internet Era*, journalist John Cassidy wrote: "What started out as a novelty for computer science major and Silicon Valley mavericks was now a staple of the MBA curriculum. The University of Michigan Business School started a course, 'From Idea to IPO in 14 weeks,' in which students developed their own start-up proposals, and a venture capital firm paid twelve thousand dollars to sit in on the class."[2]

Although they'd spent the better part of two years building Akamai, Leighton and Lewin still harbored similar, long-term life plans of a quiet, cerebral career in academia. Suddenly, though, they were at the helm of a breakout company moving at a breakneck pace.

And both of them, despite the confidence they exuded, were in over their heads. "It's kind of like when a lobster gets boiled," explained Leighton. "You don't realize what's happening to you. You don't look in from the outside and think, 'Oh, my life has really changed.' I was too immersed and drawn in by the task at hand."

Lewin told *The Jerusalem Report*, "It's frightening. I have this company of one hundred ten people, headed by one of the biggest businessmen around with lots of money in the bank, and I'm just a graduate student."

For the professor and the student, it was a swift, unlikely journey from ivory tower obscurity to breakout star of the boom. But Leighton and Lewin were in it together, and the experience only cemented a friendship that began with an awe-struck student in pursuit of a preeminent professor. They were not just business partners; they were best friends.

Leighton's wife, Bonnie Berger, recalled: "I remember Danny bringing a sparkle to Tom's eyes. Danny brought out the best in everyone he touched." Berger recalled her amazement when, on a trip with Danny, Anne and their sons to her mother's home in the Berkshires in western Massachusetts, the first thing Lewin did when they arrived was to borrow a motorbike from the garage and set off at top speed up a nearby mountain with no charted pathways. More than an hour later Lewin returned, brimming with enthusiasm despite the fact that he'd encountered an allergen that caused his face and hands to swell up and red blotches to appear on his skin. "It was so much like Danny to start a vacation by getting on this bike and riding off," Berger said. "He was not going to come in the house and just sit there, no way. He had to charge away and see the terrain."

Lewin and Leighton shared a desk at the office and spent more time together than they did apart. Despite their shared apprehension, many business skills came to both of them naturally, but in very different ways. Leighton was a quiet force, but always one to be reckoned with. Colleagues still say that, underneath his professorial airs and reserved nature, Leighton is a fiercely competitive spirit. Todd Dagres of Battery Ventures said Leighton's greatest asset was, and still is, his brain. "He was always the smartest guy in the room," remarked Dagres. "He and Danny were such a good compliment to each other because Tom was much more level-headed and less emotional. He was just as passionate and driven as Danny, but he was there to calm him down when he'd get all worked up about something."

From the start, George Conrades, who first met Leighton and Lewin when he worked at Battery Ventures, noticed Leighton's mathematical mind working in ways few people could understand—except maybe Lewin. "Business was foreign to him, but he got really good at [it] quickly because he used that prodigious intellect," Conrades said. "He could keep the firm's balance sheet in his head like an algorithm. If one change was made he'd say, 'That's going to cost you two cents a share,' while it would take anyone else two weeks at their computers to figure it out."

Lewin quickly assumed the role of Akamai's rallying force: the indomitable, often fanatical chief technologist who approached his leadership with the intensity and determination of an army captain. Unable to contain his physical prowess, even in an office setting, Lewin rarely sat still. When he became excited or upset, he strode boldly up and down the rows of cubicles, swinging his large arms and reaching out at employees to tap them on the head, offer up a high-five, or encircle them in a hug. Sometimes his antics were sophomoric; he played office pranks, like tossing pieces of candy at people across the boardroom table and duct-taping a colleague to his desk chair. When he was mad, everyone knew. Not because he was mean, but because he so often put on theatrical displays of anger like slamming his head against the wall, putting someone in a head lock, or shouting out an exaggerated threat to the competition (a favorite was "We'll rip their hearts out!").

Beneath the histrionics, however, Lewin also possessed business savvy. Much of it came from his experience in the Israeli army, a place where he learned to function well as part of a team under even the most trying circumstances. "We all knew that when Danny [laid] down a certain direction, we were supposed to follow it, even if the timeline was incredibly short or challenging," said Jeff Young, director of corporate communications for Akamai. "You wanted to get it done. You'd think about how much work it was going to be, but then you'd think about the fact that Danny hadn't slept in three days and figure, if he hasn't slept, the least I can do is work harder... You just had this feeling that, if you could just follow this guy, you were going to be set."

Lewin was also candid about the fact that he still had a lot to learn. "He had the wisdom to know that he didn't know everything," said Laura Malo, longtime executive assistant at Akamai and the company's third female employee. "As the business grew, rapidly, there was a lot of interaction with big CEOs of companies and Danny would have to meet with these people, so he learned over time to sort of calm down and listen to them and sort of wait for a response before really making his point." Malo added: "But then, when he would come [out] of the meetings, he'd whisper something like, 'We're gonna kill 'em!'"

With the same energy he used to push the soldiers in his unit to scale a cliff or walk twenty-four hours through the desert, Lewin pushed the employees at Akamai. One of his favorite phrases, which he bellowed out to almost everyone in the office, was "You're behind!" To anyone who knew Lewin, it was not an admonition. Instead, it was his way of reminding people of their potential. It also had the added benefit of keeping people in the office at all hours, every day of the week. No one at Akamai wanted to be behind—not even one step.

Lewin's rowdy leadership style did, however, meet with some resistance. With his fervor and frankness, Lewin was entirely capable of offending people. Sef Kloninger, an engineer who joined Akamai before its official launch, described a standoff with Lewin, who ordered Kloninger to rush a project, no matter how "architecturally ugly" the result would be. "I did not want to do the ugly thing," said Kloninger, "He forced me to do it; he basically said shut up and do it—he pissed me off a bit." But Kloninger didn't stay mad. The system ended up running well for a decade, and Kloninger took away a valuable lesson: "Sometimes you just need to get things done, even if they're not pretty."

Kloninger said that if there was one thing Lewin lacked, it was the ability to humor people he didn't deem worthy of his time. "There were some people on my development team who felt like he didn't want to be bothered with them and that he talked over or around them," he explained. "He didn't suffer fools. In that sense, he was not always the best manager." Kloninger noted that he quickly grew habituated to Lewin returning from a business trip and charging up to Kloninger and his team with vigor: "He'd say, 'We need to do this, and we need to do it by tomorrow.'" Kloninger added, "I didn't like Danny at the time, because he'd often just order us to stop what we were doing and do something else. If you protested, he'd say we needed to do what was best for the company."

Kloninger said Lewin was also notorious for making promises to deliver services to customers that Akamai had not yet built. "He'd put a customer on hold and yell out, 'Can we do this by Thursday?' But before anyone even answered he'd say, 'Yes, we can do it by Thursday.' It was tough, but we ended up getting most of what he promised done." In part, this was an Israeli trait: "When you ask an Israeli if they can do something, they never hesitate and say, 'Um, I don't know how' or "I can't,'" said Marco Greenberg. "Israelis just say they can and figure it out."

For most employees, the around-the-clock commitment to the company came easily. In addition to the looming prospect of an IPO, the atmosphere in the office was often exhilarating. Every day seemed to mark another milestone. Most of Akamai's employees spent more time at 201 Broadway than they did at home, staying until all hours of the night and returning early the next morning juiced up on coffee and the adrenaline of being at the center of the boom. "All of these amazing things were happening and you wanted to be there," said John Sconyers. "You never knew what would happen, but you knew if you weren't there you might miss it."

The heart of Akamai's headquarters was, and still is, the Network Operations Command Center, known internally as the NOCC. The NOCC still looks like something out of NASA command—a dimly lit room filled with banks of flickering computers. Larger screens line its walls, displaying what appear to be impressive numbers like "1,507,193 hits per second." From the NOCC, Akamai boasts a bird's-eye view of global Internet traffic; at the time, it was a perspective no one else in the world could boast. In that one room, the company has the capacity, using data from its global network, to gather information about congestion before most ISPs even know traffic is mounting. The center of the NOCC is a digitally rendered image of a spinning globe, which twinkles with thousands of tiny lights resembling stars, each one representing a city where Akamai has servers in one or more locations.

Outside the NOCC, Akamai's home at 201 Broadway was nondescript—clusters of cubicles and offices—but it had all the trappings of the trendy startup. MIT whiz kids who were barely old enough to order a beer came to work on rollerblades and skateboards. Every Thursday, a delivery truck pulled up and stocked the kitchen with Ben & Jerry's ice cream, popcorn, soda, and frozen pizzas. A group of programmers, otherwise known as the "Java Weenies" for their caffeine-fueled all-nighters, spent their time producing the interface and graphics for the system and taking naps in a hammock suspended from the ceiling. Will Koffel, a student at MIT, was one of them. He recalled juggling the coursework for his dual degree at MIT with a part-time job at Akamai, where he worked the overnight shift overseeing operations in the NOCC. Koffel would attend class from 8:45 a.m. to 4:00 p.m., study from 4:00 p.m. to 7:00 p.m., and work at Akamai from 9:00 p.m. until 5:00 a.m. "My rule was that if I fell asleep before the sun rose, then it wasn't an all-nighter," related Koffel. He said Lewin was in the office so often and at such odd hours that he finally began to wonder if he ever slept at all. One night, he recalled, Lewin was at the office at 3:00 a.m. in what Koffel called "Field Marshal mode," coordinating all kinds of efforts and keeping everyone awake and on track. Koffel asked him, "Danny, how long have you been here?" Lewin replied: "Three days." When Koffel expressed his surprise and asked him what his secret was, Lewin told him a story about his time in the army, when his commanders would make everyone in his unit stand in full gear and a backpack for twenty-four hours straight. Every time someone would flinch or collapse, they'd add another hour to everyone's time.

Koffel said the office was "hopping" at all hours, with people rolling around in office chairs from one desk to another, tossing footballs, and microwaving a seemingly endless supply of burritos. "We'd be microwaving all night," he said. "There was just so much energy that you didn't even realize how exhausted you were." It was not uncommon to see two employees tossing a Frisbee across the room or playing miniature golf on a makeshift par-seven course set up between a few desks. The atmosphere at Akamai was so fun and so intoxicating that it became easy for people to lose track of time within its walls.

Melanie Wynkoop was one of the first few women to join Akamai's sales group. At age twenty-six, she came to interview when the company had fewer than one hundred people after hearing about Akamai's young founder who was being compared to the likes of Bill Gates, but with more charisma. She came from Price Waterhouse Coopers. "I read about the company and its background, and when I came to interview, I'd never seen anything like it," she recalled. "It was small, booming, and fabulous." Wynkoop arrived just as the sales craze began, the company securing contracts by the dozens. "It was almost like we were order takers," she noted. Despite the rush, Wynkoop said Lewin always pushed the sales staff. "He'd come to sales meetings and say, 'You people suck,'" she said. "But he wasn't trying to be mean, he was just going for the jugular. That's what he did."

But if Akamai was lacking anything, it was a chief executive officer. The company was growing exponentially, gaining customers by the handfuls and generating buzz as the next big thing, but none of this guaranteed success. For any Internet company, the paradox of making it in the dot-com boom was that, in order to survive, businesses had to explode onto the scene and keep growing rapidly; but the very pace that brought them to the top could take them out in one fell swoop. Akamai needed a seasoned executive at the controls, one with enough experience and battle scars to maintain calm in the boardroom, keep an eye to the long-term forecasts, and steer them through the inevitable ups and downs. The median age of the company's employees was thirty, and many, including three of the company's top executives, had come straight from academia. Akamai needed an elder statesman.

Leighton recalled having a conversation with Lewin early on about the top role, which either of them could have easily assumed. Lewin didn't want to be CEO, but said he'd work for Leighton if he wanted the job. Leighton said he didn't want the job, but that he would work for Lewin if he did. This set off a formal search for a CEO that, by the spring of 1999, was well into its third month. A top executive search firm regularly sent candidates to Cambridge, but when it came time to decide on someone to fill the job, Lewin couldn't commit. The reason, Leighton said, was that Lewin had already decided on the man for the job. In fact, he'd made up his mind before Akamai even incorporated, drafting a list of dream CEOs for his dream company. Topping the list was George Conrades.

At age sixty, Conrades was comfortably settled into a plumb job as a Venture Partner at Polaris. After four decades on the frontlines of two of the most successful computing companies—International Business Machine (IBM) and Bolt, Beranek, and Newman (later BBN Technologies)—Conrades had retired from the career-climbing race. Or so he thought.

Conrades first laid eyes on a computer as a student in math and physics at Ohio Wesleyan University. Conrades, who graduated from the university in 1961, was then somewhat of a star on the university's campus. Handsome and charismatic, he served as president of both his fraternity and the student body. He played the drums in a rock 'n' roll band, which he described as "full of testosterone," and spent a lot of time in the physics lab trying to blow things up. But Conrades was also a standout student with a gift for both math and physics. So when the head of the school's math department decided to offer a computing course, Conrades signed up. Before he knew it, he'd learned to program one of IBM's earliest models, the 650. In his day, Conrades said, "No one had even heard of computers." With a love for motorcycles, hot rod cars, and "anything that moved," Conrades said that he took one look at the colossal machine—with its blinking red lights and rotating magnetic drum—and fell in love. With its relatively low cost and ease of programming, the 650 was marketed as a teaching computer to science and engineering schools across the country.[3] Conrades became so skilled at programming that, before he graduated, some of the faculty members at Wesleyan approached him with a list of computer companies, including IBM, Honeywell, and NCR (National Cash Register Company). "They told me that I should interview at every one of them, and that I should be in technical sales," Conrades remembered. "I told them that I really wanted to make it as a rock star."

Reason prevailed, however, and Conrades landed an entry-level job at IBM, which by the 1960s had burgeoned into a $1 billion business. Conrades began as a systems engineer, and at the same time earned an executive MBA from the University of Chicago School of Business. Over the course of 31 years, he rose up through the ranks at IBM to become senior vice president of IBM North America, a $24 million business. In 1992, after a dispute with then-chairman of IBM John Akers, Conrades left the company. By 1994, he had become president and CEO of BBN Technologies, formerly Bolt, Beranek, and Newman, the technology and research firm that helped build ARPANET. When Conrades joined BBN, the company was a think tank that survived on government contracts. Conrades leveraged the tremendous brainpower at BBN to transform the company into one of the world's largest Internet Service Providers. In 1997, GTE Corporation* purchased BBN for $616 million, or $29 a share, more than double the stock's value when Conrades came aboard. But the corporate culture of GTE didn't agree with Conrades, and after a year spent as the president of GTE Internetworking, he left and took a year off work for the first time in his career. Conrades could have comfortably retired, but he soon realized that slowing down was not for him, or his wife, Patsy, whom he met in college. "One day, I opened the freezer and suddenly everything was falling out—chicken and steak all over the place," recalled Conrades. "And Patsy looked at me and said,

*GTE Corporation was formerly General Telephone & Electronics Corporation (1959-1982).

'George, stay out of my freezer. And get a job.'" The fact was, Conrades had spent too much time at the forefront of the digital age to sit on the sidelines of the dot-com craze. He wanted to play a part in the next big thing, so he looked to venture capital, which he said was raising its head in anticipation of the digital gold rush. In August 1998, he joined Polaris.

That summer, Conrades first made the acquaintance of Lewin and Leighton, agreeing to meet them at the suggestion of Battery's Todd Dagres. Conrades recalled sitting through the pitch session and thinking that, as much as he liked the idea, he was initially uncertain about Akamai's business model. "I understood what they were saying—not at the level of the algorithms—but about making the Internet feasible for e-commerce and robust audio and visual interaction," Conrades explained. "I lived the problem at BBN, even though we threw a lot of money at it. That's when I learned that you can't throw enough money at the Internet to make it work right." By the end of the meeting, however Conrades was so impressed with Akamai's solution that he felt Polaris had a potential gold mine. He helped convince Polaris to invest in Akamai, and decided to put in some money of his own, too. According to Conrades, his investment strategy was informed by four basic elements: the idea's greatness, the technology's potential impact, the business model's strength and, most importantly, the employees' overall caliber. For Conrades, the people always came first. As for Akamai, he had no concerns about the people. Then he considered the idea. To him, the concept of what he called an "agnostic" network—one that provided a synoptic view of the Internet—was brilliant. "It was a big idea," Conrades said. "That's a word I use for something that's not incremental in its impact, but transformative. They were promising a better Internet."

When Polaris put $4 million into Akamai's first round of financing, Conrades agreed to sit on the company's board. At the time, he had no idea that Lewin had a plan to lure him into the role of Akamai's CEO. "It was a whole seduction to get George," recalled Leighton. "Of course we knew he wouldn't be our CEO on day one, so Danny worked to get him on our board. Then we got him on the board and kept working on getting him as CEO." Conrades knew Akamai was actively searching for a CEO, but was unaware of Lewin's subtle efforts to court him. So when Lewin and Leighton invited him for breakfast at Harvest restaurant in Cambridge in late March 1999, Conrades wasn't expecting them to offer him Akamai's top job. "We told him point blank, we need you to be CEO—what's it going to take?" remembered Leighton.

Conrades laid out some terms, and Lewin said they'd get back to him later that day. On the way home from lunch, Leighton noted, instead of celebrating what was sure to be a win for Akamai, Lewin suggested they push back on Conrades's terms. "I'm driving away from the restaurant, and Danny is saying how he wants to negotiate," observed Leighton. "I said, 'Danny, what are you doing? Just say yes!'" Leighton added: "That was Danny, always wanting to negotiate the best possible deal."

In the end, there wasn't much negotiating, and, on April 7, 1999, George Conrades became Akamai's first CEO, a fitting position for a man who had long been associated with speed. "To me, Akamai is like Fed Ex," explained Conrades. "Fed Ex changed the game on the postal service, and we changed the game on the Internet." The media seized on Conrades's move to Akamai as another example of many seasoned executives taking chances on Internet startups in exchange for equity. Reporting on this trend, the May 1999 issue of *Forbes* singled out Conrades, Richard Frank, the ex-chairman of Walt Disney Television who signed on to head Food.com, and James Cannavino, former CEO of Perot Systems who joined the small network security firm CyberSafe. The article posed this question: "Why are these elder statesmen, with little left to prove, now pulling twelve-hour days to run baby firms barely on their second round of venture funding?" While the story speculated that such moves were motivated largely by money, Conrades said he was genuinely thrilled to assume the role at Akamai.[4] "I was still full of energy, and I thought the people were just fantastic," said Conrades.

Conrades came on board just in time for Akamai's second round of financing, led by Baker Communications Fund LP of New York. On May 7, Akamai secured $35 million total from Polaris and Battery Ventures, bringing the company's total venture funding raised to more than $43 million. Todd Dagres told the media it was more than the company needed, and a sizeable sum even for hot startup, which averaged about $20 million in a first round in the late 1990s. Yet Akamai was less than six months old, and its market value had already multiplied tenfold. The day the second round closed, Conrades issued a statement saying Akamai had sufficient capital and had no immediate plans for an additional round of equity or any private or public offering.[5] First, Conrades said he needed to step back and give order to what was the chaos of a startup company moving too fast to position itself clearly. "My job was not to understand the algorithms and technology but to build the framework of a business," Conrades observed. "We had to hire and establish a culture; it had to be codified for everyone." One of the first questions he posed to the small company was this: Akamai exists to do *what*? It seemed so simple, but, as Conrades still recalls, "there was a lot of uncertainty." With the help of everyone at Akamai, Conrades conceived of the company's list of guiding principles, which still stands true today. One of them, which he and Lewin agreed on, was never to dismiss an idea from any source without first giving it consideration. "There was a highly argumentative culture in place, which was either inspired by Danny's Israeli traits or the atmosphere at MIT," said Conrades. "That was good—we reveled in arguing assumptions. But when we did we made a point of listening to everyone." At IBM, Conrades concluded: "there was no ability to do this."

Some ideas, however, were not up for consideration, no matter how vehemently they were argued. Just after Conrades came on board, he asked Randall Kaplan—who was still working out of Los Angeles—to relocate to Boston. Kaplan pushed back. As the only employee based outside Boston, Kaplan argued that he had originally left his lucrative position at SunAmerica to join Akamai on two conditions: that he could remain on the West Coast, and that he would report to the company's CEO. Conrades offered Kaplan a second option: remain on the West Coast, but report to Earl Galleher, the VP of Sales. Kaplan refused, and decided to resign. His decision didn't go over well, particularly with Lewin. In the months leading up to Kaplan's departure, tensions between the two were beginning to mount. Although he acknowledged Lewin as one of the most brilliant and talented people he has ever met, Kaplan said he disliked him on a personal level for being what he called too "abrasive." Coworkers said Lewin came to dislike Kaplan, partly because he felt like Kaplan's heart wasn't in the company. Kaplan left the company with a very good deal for himself, one the *Wall Street Journal* referred to as "a boatload" of stock options—ones he could cash. "Even by the outrageous standards of Silicon Valley, Randall Kaplan is one lucky guy," noted the newspaper. "Unlike his ex-colleagues at Akamai—who have to wait around for four years—Mr. Kaplan already owns all of his shares." By the end of 1999, Kaplan's 2.4 million shares were worth approximately $633 million. [6]

Akamai used some of its new funds for hiring, or, as Lewin told reporters, "a massive mind-suck from America's top universities," to create a sixty-person research and development group. In the process, Akamai fended off complaints from a few MIT professors for creating such a powerful incentive for truancy. Even before Akamai's IPO, there were employees who requested a leave of absence from their undergraduate studies at MIT to work full-time at the company. They were not the first wunderkinds to prioritize computing over a conventional education: Microsoft's Bill Gates dropped out of Harvard, Apple's Steve Jobs dropped out of Reed College. And in the late '90s, with soaring markets propelled largely by Internet stocks, the tech sector became even more alluring, particularly to financially-strapped students inspired by the overnight millionaires of the time. In the late '90s, as MIT began to spawn more successful startups, Michael Dertouzos, then director of LCS, voiced his concern that faculty, or students, might "call in rich." In response, Akamai decided to take a firm line on the issue, partly because key members of its management team were also professors at MIT. To discourage overzealous undergraduates from abandoning their studies, the company instituted a strict stay-in-school policy.

They also tried to encourage those who opted to join Akamai instead of a PhD or Master's program to return to school and earn their higher degrees. But this became more of a challenge around the time of the IPO in the fall of 1999. Just months earlier, the *Wall Street Journal* ran a story by reporter Amy Marcus under the headline "Class Struggle: MIT Students, Lured To New Tech Firms, Get Caught in a Bind." The story featured the dilemma faced by Will Koffel, who was working at Akamai when he was a junior at MIT. Koffel was handed an assignment for his computer systems engineering course from one of his professors: find a way to speed up the delivery of Web pages. Koffel had been working on the problem as one of the "Java Weenies" at Akamai, yet he was bound by a non-disclosure agreement (NDA) not to reveal any specifics about the job, particularly surrounding the design and engineering of the company's technology.

The story went on to highlight some of the perils of a university-born startup:

"On many campuses, student jobs have come a long way from the days of busing tables in the cafeteria or checking the footnotes in a professor's research project. And as the payouts at Internet startups skyrocket, some of the conflicts these jobs present are as cutting-edge as the technology they develop." Marcus then noted that, while students seemed like ideal talent for a company that requires long hours and fresh, innovative minds, the hiring of too many could have a negative impact on the academic community.

"Intense schedules on the job can keep students from doing their best academic work. And when both student and teacher share a huge financial incentive to make a company a success, some professors might be tempted to look the other way when studies slip or homework gets in the way."

Koffel's studies *were* slipping a bit, and he told the reporter it was because, in many ways, Akamai had become his "real" university. "I've learned more at Akamai than I would in a classroom," he explained. He also noted that the possibility of becoming rich was "very cool."

Koffel entered MIT in 1996, the same year as Lewin, for an undergraduate degree in computer science and musical composition. On a Saturday night three years later, Koffel recalled Lewin and Seelig showed up at his door. "My dorm was in the middle of a party," he said. "The beer was flowing, and the lights were out, and they sat down on my futon and asked me to come work at Akamai." Koffel said no, he didn't want to get involved in anything that would take time away from earning his degree. Lewin looked at him with disbelief and said, "What are you talking about? We're going to make you a millionaire." As Koffel remembers it, "Danny said this like it was a *fait accompli*. Here I was, this college student just trying to get laid for the first time, and they were talking about millions of dollars."

Koffel had to approach his parents before making a decision, and said his father was displeased. "I tried to tell them that these guys were going to be big," protested Koffel. "But I was not the least bit convincing, and my dad kept shaking his head and saying I'd have so many opportunities after finishing school." Koffel signed on anyway. And he did, in fact, get very rich at Akamai. Not just after the IPO, but even from the start as a college student with a salary of more than $70,000 a year.

Akamai's remaining funds went to infrastructure and sales. Conrades knew that, to lead the company to incorporation, Akamai had to edge out the competition, which was posing an increasing threat to Akamai's business. By 1999, the term "caching" had spread from the complex world of computer science into the commercial marketplace. Its new status made sense considering the rising demand for graphics-heavy content, the growth of cable Internet access, and the doubling of user traffic every one hundred days. In just one year (from 1998–1999), total investments in the caching industry reached $675 million. And the roster of businesses built around it grew, too, more than doubling in that same year from thirteen to twenty-seven.[7] These businesses varied greatly in the types of caching services and products they offered, which meant they weren't all a concern to Akamai. But a few of them—including Sandpiper, Digital Island, and Speedera—were promising something similar enough to Akamai's service, and at a lower cost, that they were taking a clear cut of its customer base.

Of them, the name that sparked the greatest fighting spirit at Akamai was a company out of Westlake Village, California, called Sandpiper. Founded by two software engineers, David Farber and Andrew Swart, Sandpiper launched Footprint, its debut service, in

1996. When Akamai entered the scene, Sandpiper was already flush with venture capital from backers like America Online, Inktomi, and Times Mirror Corp. Like Akamai, Sandpiper was a content delivery service, meaning that it, too, used its own network of global data centers to replicate Web content and bring it closer to end users.[8]

On April 29, 1999, the business section of *The New York Times* featured a story on "rival" startups Akamai and Sandpiper. The reporter, Andrew Pollack, did call Akamai the "most promising" of the two, crediting its "secret" software, meaning the proprietary algorithms developed by Lewin and Leighton.[9] Less than two months later (June 17), the contest between Akamai and Sandpiper was elevated to a "dead heat" by the *Wall Street Journal*, which reported, "Akamai boasts that its technology is better than Sandpiper's and that it has more servers deployed around the Internet than its slightly older competitor. But analysts say it's too early to call a winner among the two."[10] In a similar *Forbes* article entitled "Speed Racer," Adam L. Penenberg noted that, for whichever company came out ahead, the windfall was likely to be impressive: "The outposts will happily pay millions of dollars a year if it means the *clickerati* will stick around longer because they don't have to sit, drumming their fingers in despair, as they wait for pages to unfurl on the screen."[11]

Thus, Sandpiper stood as Akamai's worthiest competitor because its business model bore several similarities to Akamai's model. Both companies sold a service that ran on server networks spanning numerous ISPs, and both rewrote URLs to redirect traffic to their own systems. In the late 1990s, Sandpiper had servers in twenty network centers operated by AOL, Sprint, and Earthlink, and had a customer list that included E! Online and WebRadio.com. Both Akamai and Sandpiper were promising more than one thousand servers by the end of 1999.

The difference between the two startups were highly technical. Sandpiper's Footprint, for example, allowed users to choose from numerous content distribution options—some simple, some advanced—for different parts of a Web site, while Akamai's FreeFlow optimized everything automatically. While Sandpiper's technology never proved itself as fast and efficient as Akamai's, the company had some bragging rights of its own. For instance, it kept *The Starr Report* available on the *Los Angeles Times* site when many others buckled, and served the software company Intuit's site reliably all through tax season. Also, Sandpiper's sales team was fast-working enough to give Akamai more than a few scares. Sagan remembered a couple of sales calls to potential clients that were just days, maybe even hours, too late. "We'd arrive and the person we were meeting with would have a Sandpiper mug on their desk," he said.

In some ways, Lewin loved the competition. He hated losing, yet he reveled in exploiting the rivalry with Sandpiper to motivate Akamai's sales team. As Sandpiper's fortune rose, Lewin grew increasingly obsessed with obliterating it. Dubbing the company "Sandpooper" or "Sandpecker," he fired off interoffice e-mails filled with exaggerated threats to its existence like ripping out its heart. At one point, George Conrades felt Lewin had gone a little too far, asking him to cease the crude references to Sandpiper. But Lewin could never really bring himself to stop completely. For as long as Sandpiper posed a threat, he carried on in a slightly subtler manner in his e-mails, referring to the maiming and crushing of unnamed small birds.

It wasn't just Akamai's technology that won over some of the most enviable companies on the Internet; Akamai also had a distinct advantage when it came to customer service. It wasn't unusual for a customer to call the NOCC at 3:00 a.m. about a slowdown in service only to get a call back from Lewin or Leighton. "If the customer had a problem, they were immediately available," said Galleher. "That's not like a lot of founders who get arrogant and don't want to hear about anything going wrong." What's more, the customer calling wouldn't just get an inexperienced hired hand on the line or a temp taking a message. Most of the time, a PhD candidate from MIT was monitoring the NOCC while perhaps reading about game theory.

By June 1999, Akamai had serious bragging rights. The company had twenty of the most popular Web sites as customers—including CNN Interactive, GO Network, About.com, Infoseek, Yahoo, *The New York Times,* and The Motley Fool—and more than six hundred servers on more than twenty networks. It also boasted a Board of Advisors of prominent names including Tim Berners-Lee of W3C, music and movie legend Gil Friesen, and CNN's Sam Gassel.[12]

All of this made marketing Akamai a thrill for Jeff Young, who joined the company that month as its head of public relations. Until that time, the job had fallen on Marco Greenberg and Wendy Ziner, a smart, spirited young woman who was the first full-time hire for marketing. But Akamai's profile was rising and with it the media requests were intensifying. Young had been working in PR for Nortel Networks when he first heard about Akamai. He interviewed at the company, and when he received an offer, Young leapt at the chance to live the dot-com life for a while like so many of his peers. On his first day of work, Young was at the office until 11:30 p.m. "I thought, 'What have I gotten myself into?'" Young recalled, describing his first impressions of the crazy hive of activity, where employees, after working long hours, were sleeping under their desks or riding scooters through the halls. But Young, too, fell under the spell of Akamai. Before he knew it, he was spending countless late nights at the office, juggling a whirlwind of press releases announcing partnerships, strategic alliances, new services, and customers. In addition, "I was getting dozens of calls a day from reporters," Young said. "The story was incredible, and in a lot of ways, it sold itself." Despite this, Lewin drove Young, too. "He wanted more press," Young explained.

In late June, Young and his coworkers delivered and executed a big idea—one that was expensive but also one they wagered could end up paying for itself. In an unusual move for a startup, Akamai purchased two entire pages of ad space in the *Wall Street Journal*. On the left side, the ad read, "THERE'S ONLY ONE THING FASTER THAN OUR INTERNET CONTENT DELIVERY SERVICE." And on the right, it followed with this: "THE SPEED AT WHICH COMPANIES ARE SIGNING UP FOR IT." Above the text was a cluster of twenty customer logos including Yahoo, CNN, Apple, and *The New York Times*. "It just hit you in the face when you opened the paper," noted Young. "It had tremendous impact, and said, we're open for business, and we're loud and proud." Conrades called it the ad "that took the oxygen out of the competitor's boardrooms."

There was plenty of good news in the go-go days of the boom, but no one at Akamai had much time to stop and sing their own praises. June also marked the start of a feverish sales campaign initiated by Galleher called "100 in 100." The goal was straightforward: sign one hundred customers in a one hundred–day period. Galleher pasted a list of the most desirable companies to the office wall, and designed T-shirts with the campaign slogan. The sales team hit the road. "There was so much excitement about it," said Sconyers. Every time Akamai cemented a deal, someone would ring a bell in the office. People would jump on their chairs and hoot and holler like they were ringside at a boxing match.

Akamai was growing so fast it even became challenging to staff it. With the ongoing sales race and improvements to the technology, the company was hiring like crazy—as many as fifty new people a week. Even though Akamai had taken over a whole new floor of the office building, there weren't enough cubicles to accommodate the newcomers. Some of the engineers made makeshift desks out of cardboard boxes. Akamai was so hot that it was poaching recruits from big-name consulting firms like McKinsky & Co., and most of them were accustomed to their own corner office and executive assistant. But like most startups of the time, Akamai was moving too quickly for the typical perks of huge corporations. The stark fact of startup life was that those who joined had to be willing to do everything from writing code and pitching clients to taking out the garbage. Julia Austin, one of Akamai's first female managers, remembered arriving for her first day on the job to find that her new "office" was a small table positioned by the door of a "conference" room that was packed with employees, crammed shoulder to shoulder, furiously clattering on keyboards at a shared table. Austin expressed some surprise, and, in response, someone looked at her and exclaimed, "You got your own table! What are you complaining about?"

Austin was an art major at the University of Massachusetts, Amherst with a Master's in Management Information Systems from Boston University. As the daughter of an engineer, she grew up with a love for science and anything high-tech. By the age of eight, she was learning to program computers. Austin came to Akamai from a leading healthcare company where she worked as a consultant and led an information technology team. She later described the experience of walking into Akamai on her first day as "pandemonium." Austin managed a team of young engineers who were brilliant, but at times, their youth and inexperience made them cocky and hard to manage. "At the time, I felt like I was the adult," said Austin, who was quickly promoted to the job of VP of Engineering. Austin said Lewin was also prone to outbursts when things went wrong: "He would yell at me, and I'd just tell him to call me when he was ready to have a grown-up conversation." Austin said she'd often see an eraser or some office object fly past her head as she marched out of Lewin's office. Austin was one of just a few full-time working mothers at Akamai. With two young kids at home, Austin found it difficult to keep Akamai's crazy work hours. But like most of her co-workers, she was somehow inspired enough to keep pace. "I felt like I'd sold my soul," she remarked. "But the truth was that I wanted to be there. That's what it was like at Akamai; there was just nowhere else you wanted to be."

That same summer in 1999, a whiz kid named Mike Afergan joined Akamai. Afergan was a student at Harvard, where he was studying the application of game theory to network systems. On his first day, Afergan arrived with the expectation that he'd spend a few hours getting situated, setting up a desk and an e-mail account or filling out paperwork. Instead, Lewin called him into a meeting that included some of Akamai's top brass. It was slightly unnerving, but also exciting, so Afergan took a seat and listened eagerly as Lewin addressed the room. In July, Lewin said, Akamai would be participating in the largest streaming media event in the history of the Internet. Akamai's partner in this event was Apple, and the featured speaker would be Steve Jobs. Jobs was using the event as a platform to launch the company's QuickTime TV. The meeting quickly turned into a discussion about how the technology of Akamai and Apple would work together, and how Akamai would build it. Afergan remembered thinking he was in way over his head. Toward the end of the meeting, Lewin raised the question of who would take charge of the event, but there were no takers—no one had the time. Lewin looked over at Afergan. "How about the new guy?" he asked. Stunned, Afergan stammered something like, "I'm happy to help in any way I can, but I know nothing about your technology or anything about the company. I don't know anything." Lewin stared right back at him, and replied: "You *will* know."

On July 7, 1999, Steve Jobs debuted Apple's QuickTime TV (QTV)—at the MacWorld Expo in New York. It was a blockbuster event, and the architecture for its live stream, which Afergan helped design, ran perfectly. To a crowd of approximately five thousand, Jobs, then Apple's interim CEO, said, "On the Internet, there is so much traffic now that if you're trying to receive a broadcast in New York that's being broadcast in California, (with) live streaming on the Internet, it doesn't work so well . . . It gets interrupted quite a bit . . . The quality is quite low . . . There's no guaranteed transmission rates . . . So the experience is not so terrific." To make it terrific, Jobs said, Apple had a new partner. "Apple and Akamai are working together to build a global network that will deliver the highest quality streaming video and audio over the Internet." Jobs explained that Apple would integrate its QuickTime player and streaming server technology with Akamai's global Internet content delivery service, and that Akamai would be the company's exclusive network provider for QTV. For Akamai's part, Conrades issued a statement promising the partnership would elevate streaming media "to a new level of performance not yet realized on today's Internet."[13]

The market for streaming media was in full swing. It was still a new medium, and one that typically functioned poorly—online video was then characterized by constant freezes, blurriness, or distorted sound. This made it open territory for domination in a new digital market. Rivaling Apple's QTV was RealNetwork's Real Player, which also worked on both Macs and Windows PCs. Apple was banking on the hope that, eventually, content providers would make the switch to QuickTime because it would position the company as a leader in the streaming category.[14]

Now in a high-profile partnership with Apple, Akamai's public profile was growing well beyond the U.S. On July 5, *The Jerusalem Report* ran a splashy feature on Lewin titled "The Brain that Beat the World Wide Wait." The story began with a nod to Lewin's physical strength, but quickly shifted focus. It read: "Danny Lewin works out three times a week, and you can see the results: He's built like a linebacker. But it's in high-tech that the former Jerusalemite is an up-and-coming all-star. In fact, he's the brain behind a company that experts say is set to change the face of the Internet forever."

The story marked the first and only time Lewin agreed to participate in any significant media coverage of himself, or Akamai, and the reporter noted his discomfort: "Lewin's role in all this, and his unexpected entry into the upper echelons of American business, embarrasses him, makes him giggle and poke fun at himself. A year ago, he confesses, he didn't know the difference between a chief financial officer and a chief operating officer."[15] The story made its way to Lewin's family in Jerusalem, who modestly tucked it away with what would later become a hefty stack of stories about Danny, Akamai, and his contribution to the Internet. Charles and Peggy Lewin still insist that, to them, Danny's success came as no surprise. "From the very beginning, Danny thought he was going to take over the world," said Peggy Lewin. "As soon as they got their funding, we didn't think about whether Danny was going to be a success or not. Danny knew he was going to be a success, and he transmitted that confidence to everyone around him."

By late summer, Akamai had reached the one hundred sales in one hundred days goal set by Earl Galleher with new customers including Bluefly, CBS, eBags, GO Network, Martha Stewart Living, and Monster.com. But August—typically a quiet month—brought even better news.

Akamai was featured in a flattering article in *WIRED* magazine under the headline "The New Cool." Journalist Paul Spinard began the story with the lines "Paul Sagan said that Danny could leave the company to finish his PhD and publish his thesis, but then they'd have to kill him. Everyone else at Akamai is encouraged to complete their academic work, a slew of them at MIT, but Danny—they'd have to off him. He knows too much." Spinard went on to liken Akamai's technology to great historic shifts like the invention of Arabic numerals or the development of seafaring. Spinard wrote, "Tom and Danny knew with total certainty that, given their descriptions of the hot spot problem and the workings of the Net, the larger the network grew, the better their solution would perform. They not only had a solution, they had a solution that was literally—demonstrably—unbeatable." Spinard then outlined Akamai's competition, most notably Sandpiper, and ended the piece on the following note: "Either way you look at it, the stakes are high. The winner, if there is one, will have its hand in the major revenue-generating sites on the Web. More than any other company in the medium's short history, the winner will own the Net—or at least the parts of it that pay."[16]

Akamai made headlines again when it entered into a strategic partnership with Cisco Systems, a worldwide leader in Internet networks, to optimize its content delivery service. Weeks later, Microsoft invested approximately $15 million in Akamai and partnered with the company to integrate its new software technologies into Akamai's network. It had been less than a year since Lewin visited the Seattle headquarters of Microsoft to try to secure a meeting with an executive there. He was turned away, and when he refused to leave the building, he had to be physically escorted out. The next day, undeterred, Lewin returned. "Some people did try to say no to Danny," recalled Leighton. "It just never lasted very long."

On August 20, Marco Greenberg sent an e-mail to Lewin: "Let me congratulate you on a most significant and exciting week in Akamai's history. The announcement of deals with Cisco and Microsoft are incredible, and you deserve an enormous amount of credit in making it all happen."

Boosted by Akamai's recent string of victories, Earl Galleher set a new, bolder sales goal: two hundred new customers by December 31. Galleher was fired up, but Paul Sagan was doubtful that the company could continue to grow its customer base at such a frenzied rate. "Sagan said to me, 'No way,'" Galleher recalled. "So I told him, 'I'll prove it to you, and if I make it, then you will have to get up and dance in a hula outfit before the management team.'" Sagan shook on it.

CHAPTER 9

Overnight Zillionaires

"The way to become rich is to put all your eggs
in one basket and then watch that basket."

— ANDREW CARNEGIE

In June 1999, after six months in business, Akamai had no profit-ability and a deficit of $10.8 million. It did have revenues of around $400,000, but 89 percent of it came from just two customers, Apple and Yahoo (75 percent from Apple, and 14 percent from Yahoo).[1] But at the time, no one really cared—the markets were in the grips of irrational exuberance. "The valuations have never been this outlandish, the participation quite this democratic, or the market quite so resistant to what always used to work," wrote financial reporter Pete Barlas for *Investor's Business Daily*.[2] In 1998, Internet IPOs raised $1.3 billion. By the end of 1999, that number had risen to a record $16.9 billion from 214 Internet companies, more or less at the rate of one IPO a day.[3]

By the summer of 1999, despite the fact that Akamai had only been in existence for less than a year, market watchers were busy predicting the timing of its IPO. Rumors abounded that the company had filed a registration statement with the Securities and Exchange Commission (SEC). The message boards of The Motley Fool featured lengthy discussion threads under the heading: "Akamai IPO?"

Even a year earlier, no one would have been talking about taking a tiny, largely unproven Internet infrastructure company like Akamai public so soon after its inception. Against the backdrop of a market that was experiencing frequent gains of more than 100 percent from IPO investing, however, the time frame from when a company got its first venture-capital financing to when it launched an IPO dramatically decreased.[4] Bankers were racing to sell deals as soon as they could pull them together, and the pace would continue as long as the market allowed. The shrinking timetable made some investors, and some of the executives at Akamai, slightly anxious. To push toward an IPO with no profits seemed almost reckless, but Akamai had a story to sell; a compelling one. "It's true that the company had very little revenue," said Todd Dagres of Battery. "But they convinced Wall Street that they were a unique company, a leader in a new category, and that they had the potential for huge growth. It was a sexy story."

That summer, the big banks started to court Akamai. In a series of back-to-back, hour-long meetings commonly referred to in the industry as the "bake off" or "beauty contest," Akamai met with teams from twenty investment banks, each vying to lead the IPO. One in particular stood out, largely because of its leader. Chris Pasko, a thirty-four-year-old Harvard MBA, had moved to Boston in 1996 to open a new office for Morgan Stanley Dean Witter (now just Morgan Stanley) to target the region's tech boom. Pasko said he didn't love the technology per se, but he loved entrepreneurs. Likening his job to a pro football coach scouting college players for the NFL, Pasko said he met with several hundred up-and-comers every year—one after another promising big ideas and big gains. Of them, he had an eye for the best; he'd worked at Morgan Stanley early in the decade and saw the potential in companies like AOL when it had just 100,000 subscribers. Pasko had been flirting with Akamai since the start of the year, when he first met with Lewin and Leighton. After that, he spent as much time as possible with the two of them in an effort to understand how Akamai worked. "It was the most complex technology I had ever seen," said Pasko. Of all the companies he scouted that year, Pasko and his team would take approximately five public, and they were determined to make Akamai one of them. The Akamai "bake off" took place over two days in July. By the time Pasko and his team made their pitch, Akamai's executives had sat through about twenty hours of pitches from twenty prominent banks including Goldman Sachs and Credit Suisse. Pasko knew he needed to do something to stand out. "No matter how good you are, there's always the chance that you'll get lost in the shuffle," Pasko said. The day of the meeting, he made a snap choice that could have backfired in a room full of techies and businessmen; Pasko went out and bought Hawaiian shirts for his team members, instructing all eight of them to wear them instead of suits. Pasko said he knew the shirts were a hit the minute he walked into the conference room and saw everyone grinning. "They were a loud, larger-than-life group, and they loved the shirts," Pasko said. They also loved the presentation, which reflected a profound understanding not only of Akamai's technology, but also of its market potential. It was a winning combination of quirkiness and intelligence; Akamai chose Pasko and his team at Morgan Stanley Dean Witter to lead the IPO, which was co-managed by Donaldson, Lufkin & Jenrette (now defunct), Solomon Smith Barney (now part of Morgan Stanley), and Thomas Weisel Partners LLC.

The next step in the IPO process is one of the most tedious—the drafting of the prospectus, a document mandated by the SEC that contains all the facts necessary for prospective investors. The drafting took days, a job Pasko said is usually left to the bankers and company financial officers. Much to Pasko's surprise, Lewin and Leighton wanted to be a part of the process, even though they'd never read a prospectus and had no idea how to write one. "Danny obsessed over that document," said Pasko. "He read dozens of prospectuses and became an expert; I've never seen a company founder get so involved."

With the prospectus complete, Pasko's team took Akamai on what's called the "road show," two weeks of traveling around the country and abroad to pitch the company's stock to financial institutions before its public offering. Again, Lewin took Pasko by surprise by insisting that he join the road show. "You don't typically see a scientist without an MBA or business experience out on the road show, but Danny was out there with us, giving the pitch," Pasko said. "It was unique, and incredibly powerful."

Like most road shows, Akamai's tour was grueling—involving full days of meetings in more than a dozen cities. But it was also a smashing success. After meeting with more than 200 financial institutions, Akamai had an order book, or a record of investors' demands for available shares, that was at least thirty times oversubscribed. In addition, every one of the sixty accounts the group met with in person put in an order for shares, making what's called the "one-on-one hit rate" 100 percent, which is exceptional. "It happens, but even then it was exceedingly rare," said Pasko.

In the weeks leading up to the IPO, Pasko and his team worked with Lewin, Leighton, and the rest of Akamai's executives to price the stock for an initial offering of ten million shares. Pricing an IPO is as much art as it is science. The basic elements are supply and demand. And in normal times, when the markets are steady, banks usually factor in a discount to protect the company of about ten to twelve percent. But these were not normal times, and even to sharp bankers like Pasko, none of the regular rules made sense. His goal, shared by Akamai, was to have the stock trade upwards, sending the message that it was hot. Pasko led Akamai through what he still considers the script for a successful IPO process, always careful to remind everyone involved that the script didn't guarantee a high-flying IPO. "Very few companies that did this back then made it long-term," Pasko said. "They all got big pops in price, but they didn't have viable business plans, and in the long haul, many of them died."

During the discussions over pricing, Leighton and Lewin asked countless questions. As mathematicians, they were frustrated by what they perceived as a lack of logic. If all the large banks were in for ten percent, couldn't they use basic math to price the stock?

Pasko reminded them of the risk of flipping: if everyone flips their shares, he told them, then the stock can tumble as much as eighty percent. (In 2012, this fate befell Facebook, which suffered a catastrophic IPO when Morgan Stanley priced its shares too high and sold too many.) "There's really no math in it," stated Pasko.

On the eve of the IPO, the Akamai team traveled to New York to set the final price of the stock, which had the Street buzzing with anticipation. That week, *Forbes* magazine speculated that Akamai would make history, calling it "poised to become one of this year's [1999] most explosive startups." By 5:00 p.m. the night before the IPO, they finished, settling on an opening price of $26 a share. In keeping with tradition, Pasko extended an invitation to everyone from Akamai to stay overnight and stand on the trading floor to ring the opening bell on the exchange and watch the first orders for Akamai's stock trade. Pasko was surprised when they declined, instead deciding to return to Cambridge and "get back to work." So Pasko traveled with them and helped arrange for a live satellite hookup in Akamai's conference room where they could watch the trades. It was the first time in Pasko's career that a company had opted *not* to be at Morgan Stanley or the NASDAQ to celebrate the first trade of their shares.

On the morning of Friday, October 29, 1999, more than one hundred employees gathered in Akamai's conference room to watch company history unfold. Anne Lewin and Bonnie Berger joined the crowd. At Lewin's urging, Pasko stood on a chair to talk everyone through the process as it happened. This was also a first for Pasko, who couldn't help but think that, at a time when most people would be focused on just how much they would soon be worth, Lewin mainly wanted to know exactly how the IPO worked. "I kept thinking, 'You're going to be really rich in about ten minutes,' but Danny saw it as another teaching moment," said Pasko.

Around 12:00 p.m., Akamai's stock (NASDAQ: AKAM) opened at $26 a share. The first trade was over $100 a share. From there, it continued to explode. Over $1 million shares were traded that day.

Cheers erupted, and glasses of champagne clinked. Lewin leapt around with excitement, while Leighton sat completely stunned, jaw agape as he watched the price continue to rise. "He was utterly shocked," said Berger.

On its first day of trading, Akamai's shares closed at $145.1875, up $119.1875, or 458 percent. That valued the company at $13.12 billion, based on the 90.4 million shares outstanding. It was the fourth-biggest percentage gain ever for an IPO.

The aftershocks of the astronomical IPO were felt far and wide. At the grillroom of the Four Season's Hotel in New York, angel investors Art Bilger, Jan Wenner, and Peter Morton had lunch to celebrate the IPO. When they got word of the first few trades, Wenner was so thrilled that he let out a yelp.

In Jerusalem, Lewin's family watched the stock trade online. They gave thanks to Danny, who had generously given them all family shares that would make them wealthy, too.

In California, Eric Lehman, Lewin's friend and classmate at MIT, saw the news of Akamai's IPO and remembered an official "friends of the company" letter he'd received months earlier from Lewin granting him some shares. He hadn't thought much of it and stuffed it in a dresser drawer. That day, he dug it up and quickly ran the math. His shares were worth over $1 million.

Akamai's public offering didn't just make history for its astronomical gains; it also created one of the most eclectic groups of overnight millionaires ever known up to that point.[5] A professor of theoretical computer science and MIT students, both full-time and part-time at Akamai, were suddenly worth more on paper than executives of blue chip companies. MIT itself reaped the rewards.

Having agreed to license the technology Leighton and Lewin created at the university in exchange for 494,000 shares of Akamai, MIT held a stake worth over $90 million.[6]

The biggest beneficiaries of it all, of course, were the co-founders: Professor Leighton and his former student, Danny Lewin. On paper, Leighton, 42, and Lewin, 29, were each worth more than $1.8 billion.[7]

Marco Greenberg, who traveled to Cambridge for the day, easily recalled the euphoria of that moment—for him, Lewin, and everyone at Akamai. "Danny knew they had fired one shot and it hit the mark—boom, like a rifle," he said. "It was a magical time. We were right there at the heart of the Internet revolution." And they were rich—crazy rich.

Lewin didn't spend much time reveling in it. Almost as soon as the crowd filtered out of the conference room, he was busy telling people to get back to work. Greenberg remembered stopping in Lewin's office before returning to New York. Lewin was already back at his desk but paused to share one of the congratulatory e-mails he'd just received. It was from Randall Kaplan, who applauded Lewin and noted that he had worked hard. Greenberg said Lewin, still angry with Kaplan for cashing out of Akamai so early, couldn't resist sending back the following: "You're right. I worked hard."

Then, in true fashion, he attended to business. A few days later, though, Lewin expressed a hint of regret for not taking more time to revel in the IPO. In an e-mail to Greenberg, Lewin wrote, "What a day Friday was … Thanks for coming to Akamai, and I'm sorry that I didn't have more time."

In the two months after the IPO, Akamai's fortunes just kept on rising. By Thanksgiving, the stock had climbed to $201 a share. Akamai doubled its customer base for FreeFlow to two hundred companies, including Bloomberg.com, CNET, Jobs.com, and Wil-liams-Sonoma.com.[8] Greenberg was being inundated with press requests for interviews with Lewin, who declined in the IPO's aftermath. An article in the December 3, 1999, edition of the Israeli newspaper *Haaretz* called Lewin "one of the richest Israelis in the world." The paper also printed a comment issued by Lewin for the country's media outlets, stating, "I wouldn't hesitate to describe myself as a proud Israeli, who is on an extended *shlichut* (mission) abroad. So while I am convinced I will return to Israel one day, currently I am devoting my time and energy to building Akamai Technologies into a global high-tech power that we hope will have a big impact on the Internet."

Lewin also hinted at a future for Akamai in Israel, noting: "I would not be surprised if one day the company considers opening an R&D facility in Israel to take advantage of the country's brainpower."[9]

At the end of the year, making good on his bet with Galleher over the sales challenge, Sagan stood up in front of the company's management team at a meeting held at the Residence Inn in Cambridge and danced in a hula outfit (grass skirt, coconut top), which he changed in and out of in the men's room. Akamai closed out 1999 with a New Year's Day stock price of $327. It made no sense, even to Pasko. It was wealth beyond anyone's wildest imagination.

With the perspective that comes with the turn of a new year, and in this case, the turn of a century, most people involved with Akamai took what little time they had over the holidays to look back on 1999 and wonder exactly what had happened. In less than one year, a tiny startup out of MIT had grown to a company with a market valuation greater than that of General Motors. What's more, it looked to most industry experts like Akamai had staying power at a time when the majority of dot-coms were already starting to report losses.

On January 3, 2000, the *New York Times* ran a column called the "Year in Markets." "In a year of Internet frenzy, paper millionaires were minted almost daily as companies without profits and often no sales issued stock to the public and watched it soar." The piece went on to say that the "most likely route to riches seemed to be creating a company that would provide services to other companies exploiting the Web. Akamai Technologies hit it right with a process to speed up delivery of content over the Internet."[10] And *The New York Post*, in its characteristically less serious style, published a feature on January 2 listing its annual predictions for the business world in a column called "The Bull's Eye." Granted, the piece made such comments as "The market goes up, the market goes down," and "Once a week, like clockwork, an Internet company nobody has ever heard of buys another Internet company nobody has ever heard of for a sum equal to the GDP of Denmark." Yet, notably, it also said the following: "Shares of…Akamai Technologies continue to rise, even though nobody has any idea what [it] does."

Everyone at Akamai lived by the stock ticker, watching their fortunes rise and fall as the markets began to froth. Those who held insider shares were bound by a lockup (no-sell) period of six months, or 180 days, during which they were prohibited from selling their shares by the SEC. Lockups are standard procedure on Wall Street, carried out to protect investors from the instability that mass selling can create. Until the lockup expired, the riches of Akamai's employees were held captive.

Akamai had fought its way to the top of content delivery— once a niche industry—and had been crowned "kings of caching" by the media and the market watchers. Its blockbuster IPO was widely viewed as a positive predictor of Akamai's long-term viability. But to anyone familiar with the dark side of dot-com wealth, there was also the risk that a rise as spectacular as Akamai's could also be too much of a good thing. "I don't think anyone really wanted to hear this, but I actually raised the idea at the time that it could actually cause tremendous problems," recalled early Akamai investor and board member Art Bilger. "I remember saying that day stocks, at least in the world I come from, don't trade like this. And the worst thing that could happen was for people inside the company to think that it was real. I don't mean the company being real, I mean the stock." Bilger had good reason to voice caution. Having seen his fair share of over-valued, over-hyped companies crash and burn, Bilger also advised Akamai's decision-makers to "make sure no one goes out and buys homes and things far beyond what they afford, because that would be terrible."

Fortunately, the corrosive culture of greed never got a widespread grip on Akamai. There were some takers—a few employees who came in, negotiated large packages, and skipped out as soon as they could cash out. But the majority of Akamai's employees at the time of the IPO seemed keenly aware of the ephemeral nature of sudden, admittedly absurd, wealth. In part, it was the staid culture of Cambridge and MIT that kept Akamai's overnight millionaires and billionaires from embarking on ostentatious spending sprees, building ten-bedroom mansions, or sporting inflated egos. Unlike the Silicon Valley startups founded out of someone's garage, Akamai had its roots at LCS, where IQ carried a lot more weight than net worth. To be sure, there was some evidence of instant fortunes—nicer cars in the parking lot, bigger homes, or vacations to tropical islands. But the majority of Akamai's employees downplayed the riches and focused on work.

On the day of the IPO, Will Koffel joined the ranks of Akamai-made student millionaires; his stake as an engineer of 100,000 shares was worth approximately $15 million on paper. But Koffel notes that he saw the money disappear almost as fast as it came to him.

"At the peak, I was worth about $35 million," Koffel said. "But then when the stock went down, I remember standing on my futon and making my first trades with my broker. Then the government took over a million, plus my broker fees. In the end, I can tell you I don't live that differently than most of my peers. I just have a nice retirement account."

After the IPO, Koffel bought himself a new car and joined a group of racing hobbyists at Akamai, built largely around the collection of fast, new cars people were buying. Koffel's was a BMW, and one of his first big purchases after the lockup period. The car was just four days old—still pristine—when he pulled out of the parking garage ramp at Akamai and heard someone shouting at him. Koffel looked to the side of the ramp and saw Lewin, who leapt onto the windshield and yelled: "Koffel, is this your car? No way is this your car, you're a kid!"

Koffel remembered, "I was terrified. Not for myself, but for the car!"

For Lewin, of course, the money meant relief from what had been a struggle for him and Anne to foot the bills for their family of four. They bought a larger home in Brookline, Massachusetts. Lewin bought a couple of motorcycles, which he rode with other motorcycle enthusiasts at Akamai, including George Conrades and executive assistant Laura Malo. During these rides, Conrades—who had long collected and ridden motorcycles—came to admire Lewin even more although he was less than half of Conrades's age. "It was fun to be around someone with that kind of intensity," Conrades said. "We'd take our bikes and go call on customers sometimes—once we rode all the way to Bell Canada. Danny loved the thrill of riding, being outdoors, and being in control of something so fast." Beyond this and his family's newfound financial security, however, Lewin showed little interest in the material gain. He made plans to reenroll at MIT to finish his PhD, a lifelong dream he never abandoned. He continued to dress in his uniform of blue jeans and buttoned-down shirts from the Gap, and carry his papers around in a backpack.

Leighton, for his part, mostly carried on as if little had changed. He remained in the same house that he, Berger, and their two kids had lived in for years, making plans to eventually remodel when work slowed down. "Danny and Tom were never, ever about the money," Berger still insists. "I mean, Danny didn't want to be poor and living in graduate school housing his whole life, but they didn't set out to make that kind of money, and they cared about the company. They wanted to see the technology work." Berger said she noticed only one discernible change in Leighton when he became a paper billionaire. "He used to keep this really organized, line-item list of every one of our expenses," explained Berger. "After the IPO, he stopped doing that."

Leighton, Lewin, and many others at Akamai looked at their paper fortunes from the perspective of sound mathematics, a discipline in which reason prevails. Everyone also knew the nature of bubbles. Eventually, they burst. And when this one did, no one wanted to be the one standing in a half-finished mansion.

"The story of our lives at Akamai is that we never had much time to stop and think," said Leighton. "Even after the IPO, we got together for an hour or so and then said, 'Let's get back to work.'" And they did. On the night of the IPO, Leighton remembered staying up until well after midnight e-mailing all of the company's customers to reassure them that the wild IPO did not mean that anyone at Akamai would become lazy for one second. Lewin himself barely paused that day, barking at his colleagues that, despite the events of the day, they were still "behind!"

In the wake of the IPO, Akamai faced a daunting challenge: living up to it. The company was confronted with newer, grander expectations from analysts and brand new investors. It had to grow, and it had to do so rapidly. Before the end of January, Akamai had launched its European Operations with headquarters in Munich, Germany, and offices in London and Paris. To run it, the company hired the former general manager of BBN Europe, Wolfgang Staehle, as president of Akamai Europe. Staehle had more than two decades of experience in high-tech sales and management, leading not only BBN, but also IBM Deutschland gmbH. Akamai also opened an office in San Mateo, California, partly to be in close proximity to some of its biggest accounts, such as Apple and Yahoo, but also to tap into the talent of Silicon Valley.

Akamai also looked to become a leader in streaming media. Many streaming media companies were plagued by the same content delivery issues that brought Akamai into being: hot spots and lack of bandwidth. With its distributed architecture, Akamai was well positioned to take the lead. Its first major move in that direction was the acquisition of InterVu, Inc., a San Diego-based Internet audio and video service provider, on February 7, 2000 in a $2.8 billion stock swap. The deal turned Akamai into an instant streaming media giant with over one thousand of the Web's most popular sites, including major television networks and Hollywood Studios.[11] Analysts immediately praised Akamai's purchase of InterVu. Appearing on CNNFN, analyst Mark Langer of JP Morgan said, "I think it's important at this stage in its development for Akamai to continue to grow itself by acquiring potential competitors, companies in adjacent spaces. And that's exactly what InterVu provides them."[12] Weeks after the InterVu purchase, Akamai entered into an alliance with RealNetworks to deliver broadband Internet broadcast service worldwide.

Akamai wasn't done improving its foothold in streaming media, though, and it kept looking to the West Coast. InterVu wasn't based in San Diego by chance. The streaming media business was seeing the most action in California, where companies like Napster, which allowed users to download shared music, were cropping up everywhere. One of the hottest California-based startups was Farmclub.com, the brainchild of Jimmy Iovine, co-chairman of Interscope Geffen A&M, and Doug Morris, chairman and chief executive officer of Universal Music Group. Farmclub was a Web site designed to integrate television, the Web, and record labels. Farmclub encouraged unsigned musicians to upload their songs for free to its site, where they could be downloaded and audio-streamed for free. In turn, those musicians were given the possibility of fame and stardom.

To win over Farmclub, Akamai would have to again bridge the gap between Internet science and the high-wattage world of entertainment. Media mogul and Akamai board member Gil Friesen made an introduction, inviting Lewin and a few others from Akamai out to California to meet with some of Farmclub's team in the summer of 2000. Friesen recalled thinking just how much Lewin stuck out in Hollywood. Having invited Lewin to lunch at some Los Angeles hot spot, Friesen saw Lewin bounding in, dressed in his jeans and tennis shoes. In a gesture of thanks for Friesen's efforts to connect Akamai with Farmclub, Lewin dropped to the ground and pretended to bow at his feet. "No one in Hollywood does that," Friesen said.

The architect of Farmclub was Glenn Kaino, executive vice president and head of programming. Kaino was a prodigy, hired at age twenty-five by Iovine for his rare blend of sharp technological skills and artistic talent. An accomplished visual artist, Kaino also knew computer science, having studied it in college. Kaino likened his first meeting with Lewin to an arranged marriage. "It was totally forced," said Kaino, who quickly took a liking to Lewin, despite himself. "He was stiff and earnest, but had enough natural charm and charisma. I remember thinking that he was a square, super-nice guy." Kaino planned another meeting for Lewin, this one with Iovine.

In walked Lewin—jeans, t-shirt, a spring in his step—to a room full of California cool on the lot of Universal Studios. "Everyone in the room was like, 'No way is this possible,'" said Kaino. "But I remember from that moment Danny got up there and started talking that it made perfect sense; he had a direct problem, and he was approaching it in an indirect way. It was like he was walking through walls." It made sense to Kaino, but he wasn't sure about the rest of the group. Jimmy Iovine was quiet, and halfway through the meeting, Kaino noted that Lewin started directing his pitch straight to Iovine. "If Danny was insecure, he never let anyone feel it," Kaino remarked. "He never broke a sweat, and he just let loose on everyone in the room. Jimmy had no idea what the fuck he was talking about."

But Iovine didn't care. He saw something in Lewin, and he was won over. "I'm a music guy, your voice is great," Iovine said. "I don't care what you're selling, I'm buying it." Recalling that moment, Kaino said: "Jimmy was referring to the confidence, the articulation and the passion in Danny's voice… It was amazing to watch." A deal was soon put on the table, and, in September 2000, Akamai (along with a digital media company called Loudeye) signed on to provide streaming media services to Farmclub.com. To celebrate, Iovine invited Lewin to his house in Hollywood Hills, where Lewin rubbed shoulders with stars including the director James Cameron and rappers Dr. Dre and Eminem. "In some ways Danny was the perfect person to break into this industry—he was speaking a different language, but he believed in it," said Freisen. And Akamai was flourishing as a result. That spring in 2000, Akamai had expanded to over 2,750 servers in more than 150 networks in 45 countries.

No amount of growth, however, could combat the reality of the markets on the brink of the dot-com bust. On March 10, 2000, the NASDAQ closed at 5046.86 points—double the close of exactly one year earlier. The next day, though, the freefall began. Technology shares began to plunge and, with them, went scores of the Internet companies with no earnings to their trendy names. Akamai felt the tug. Within just two days, as the technology-dominated NASDAQ fell 466 points, shares of Akamai took a hit. The media immediately seized on the drop with a report on what it all meant for CEO George Conrades. CNBC anchor Ron Insana opened his broadcast with the question "Who's losing money on Wall Street?" The answer? "George Conrades," Insana said. "His company's stock was among the hard hit in the NASDAQ, falling 29.5 points. That brings his one-day loss on paper to almost one hundred and ninety-five million."[13]

By the start of April 2000, investors began pulling money from technology stocks and moving it into old-fashioned blue-chip companies. The slide continued into April. On April 11, CNBC reported that Akamai "took it on the chin" with shares falling 19 percent to close at $107.[14]

At the end of the month, on April 26, the lockup period for Akamai's insiders expired, making 82 million shares eligible for sale. With the market fluctuating wildly and speculation that it was heading south, every one of the primary shareholders knew it could well be their moment to cash out. If they didn't, they could lose millions, even billions. But redeeming a bunch of shares would also flood the market with shares of Akamai, sending the wrong message to Wall Street. If the floodgates opened, the market could see an oversupply of shares, signaling distress at Akamai. With the demise of the bull market, such scenarios were becoming more common.

The trade publication IPO reporter took note of this pivotal time, running a story that highlighted the end of Akamai's lockup: "Venture capital firms are often among the first to sell their shares when the lockup expires. That could spell trouble for stocks like Akamai, which trades at an astounding 2,700 times 1999 revenues—and that's after plunging nearly 50% in recent weeks. Akamai's lockup ends on April 25, when a potential 82.4 million shares could enter the market—and three VC's hold 21 million of those shares. Based on Akamai's average daily trading volume, it would take the market 116 days to absorb unlocked Akamai shares, according to IPOLockup.com."[15]

Leighton and Lewin met, making what was considered a risky, unusual move—they agreed to another lockup of six months to keep insiders from dumping shares on the market. To do so, they had to ask the others who had founders stock—top management and venture capitalists—to agree to do the same, waiting to sell until at least July, when the company would report second quarter earnings. By then, they knew their net worths could be wiped out, but as Leighton said, they weren't in it for the money. If they had been, neither of them would have ever agreed to such a drastic measure. "At the end of the day, we both lost fortunes because of the decision we made," Leighton concluded.

Many others did, too. One by one, Leighton and Lewin called the company's investors and asked them if they would agree to another lockup in a show of solidarity. All but one investor agreed. "It was remarkable," Leighton said. "But it was also that culture that helped us to survive. Whether times were good, or terrible, the focus was on getting the technology out there and making a difference."

For some, it wasn't an easy decision. Greenberg will never forget the day Lewin called him with the request. "You've got to do me a favor—will you sign another lockup agreement?" Lewin asked. At the time, Greenberg had approximately 180,000 shares. Moreover, unlike some of Akamai's other investors, he wasn't flush with cash. Business at NYPR was good, but by no means a sure thing. He was also expecting his second child with his wife, Stacey Nelkin. Greenberg's wealth was on paper. By signing on to another lockup, he risked loosing it all. Not sure what to make of it, Greenberg called his accountant, who told him: "You can't do it—you've got a get out of jail free pass and you should use it." But Greenberg knew he was just going through the motions. He knew he couldn't say no to Lewin. "I wouldn't be able to live with myself if I did," he related. "That was truly the priceless nature of my friendship with Danny." Greenberg called Lewin back, agreeing to another six-month lockup. With one call, Greenberg estimated that he lost approximately $25 million.

The remainder of the year was marked by ups and downs of Akamai's stock, which recovered in June but only for a moment. Sagan made the media rounds, confidently assuring analysts and jittery investors that the company remained in good health. On July 24, Sagan appeared on CNN.

Paul Sagan: "It was an ugly day for the tech sector today. We were thrilled with our results. We beat the expectations. Our revenue went to $18 million."

Bruce Francis, Anchor: "Paul, still the stock has been under pressure over the past few months. You're now trading at what would be less than a third of your all-time high. What does the market not understand about this message?"

Sagan: "I don't think the market is confused. . . . We had a, you know, really remarkable run-up in the stock, then everybody took a very sizable hair cut. Again, we don't try to predict the markets or really explain them. We're building a large company for the long haul."[16]

Success in a speculative bubble is a funny thing. It was thrilling and intoxicating in ways the country hadn't seen since the 1980s, or, some might argue, ever. But almost as soon as the bulk of that wealth was accumulated, speculation began as to when it would all end.

By the close of July, shares of Akamai fell twenty-one percent on concerns over an increase in marketing spending. Investors became concerned because the company, which by then had a global net-work of four thousand servers, said, during a conference call with analysts, that it planned to increase spending on marketing and hiring. Nitsan Hargil, an analyst at Kaufman Brothers, replied, "People are afraid that Akamai is about to turn into another one of these Internet companies that spends its way into oblivion."[17]

New customers joined, but the markets were tanking too fast to respond. At the start of September, CNNFN's Digital Jam featured guest Andrew Barret, an analyst from Salomon Smith Barney, to talk about the "high anxiety" in the tech sector. A caller phoned in a few minutes into the show with a question, to which Barret responded.

Caller: "Hi. Thank you for taking my call. My question is Akamai. What do you see in three to six months?"

Barrett: "Well, the Akamai situation in terms of the streaming side of the equation is really, really positive. Unfortunately, nobody wants to own: a) a web based stock, and b) a name they can't pronounce half the time. So this is really been one that's taken a beating."[18]

To steer the media away from their stock price, Akamai's executives issued positive news releases. One of Greenberg's last stories for Akamai, before leaving the company to focus on his own business, was about Akamai's creation of Akamai Foundation, a math foundation tailored for kids and aimed at making math more interesting and fun with a "Magic of Math" program. The story noted that employees donated amounts ranging from several hundred to more than a million dollars of their own money. Leighton served as the foundation's director.

Akamai also began preparing for the launch of EdgeSuite, its new flagship product that would enable Web sites to deliver entire pages to customers across Akamai's network of servers.[19] EdgeSuite improved on the FreeFlow service, which mostly facilitated the delivery of large, static objects such as photos, ad banners and video. With Edgesuite, customers would have guaranteed delivery of constantly changing data such as weather and stock quotes as well as blocks of news stories. EdgeSuite was scheduled for launch in December 2000, and was already in use with beta customers including Apple, Coca-Cola, Novartis, Ticketmaster, and Victoria's Secret. As soon as news of EdgeSuite got out, market watchers started speculating as to whether it could revitalize Akamai's stock market presence. Conrades told reporters the company expected the service to generate $30 million in revenue in 2001, with customers paying $40,000 a month for EdgeSuite versus $8,000 a month for the Free-Flow service.

Unfortunately, no amount of fighting could prevent the continuing stream of bad news. To close out the year 2000, Internet stocks fell 75 percent after more than doubling in 1999. And, after a record-breaking 160 percent return in 1999, shares of Akamai sank 94 percent to $21.06 in 2000. The company had lost more than 150 dot-com customers, approximately 10 percent of its base, with more losses on the horizon. "We were burning cash like mad," explained Leighton. "Our stock was clearly headed south, and the markets were tanking."[20]

CHAPTER 10

B'SIYATA DISHMAYA
(With the Help of Heaven)

"Time is too precious. A life is a moment in
a season. A life is one snowfall. A life is one
autumn day. A life is the delicate, rapid edge
of a closing door's shadow…"

—ALAN LIGHTMAN, *Einstein's Dreams*

Despite the fact that the markets were no longer betting on Akamai, company executives chose Las Vegas for their 2001 sales kickoff. To mark the official launch of EdgeSuite, they flew several dozen employees and advisors out to Sin City for a few days at the Mandalay Bay Hotel & Casino.

As VP of sales, John Sconyers said that, despite the market downturn, the mood was celebratory. Akamai had a new service, and with it the promise of new customers. They were in Vegas, and for a time, they felt like big winners. "We were just pinching ourselves," Sconyers recalled. "It was an unbelievable experience."

Employees, customers and members of the company's board were put up in swank suites and handed substantial wads of cash to gamble. Ironically, it was the only time Dwight Gibbs of the Motley Fool recalled any sort of dispute with Lewin, who insisted that Gibbs, a member of the company's customer advisory board, stay in an upscale suite. "I said I didn't like the optics ... Danny would hear none of it," Gibbs explained. "It was a mild kerfuffle, and eventually Danny won. I should have given in immediately. It would have saved us both a lot of time."

The featured event of the sales kickoff was a speech by Lewin, who announced the official launch of EdgeSuite with much fanfare. Notwithstanding the reality of the plunging markets, he was ebullient and optimistic. "Isn't EdgeSuite a crappy name?" he asked, pausing for a laugh. "Luckily, we use it to our advantage. Microsoft also told me EdgeSuite was a crappy name, but they said we also have a crappy name so [they] respect companies with crappy names. So we should keep it even though it sucks."

Lewin acknowledged the company's losses, but pumped up the mood with a reminder of how far they had come. "When markets go down, they also go up, and when the upturn comes, we can be a hundred billion dollar company. Seriously, we *can* be.

"Our attitude, which has been true since the beginning, is that we set these massive goals. Going out a year ago and saying we'll deploy thousands of servers at the edges of the Internet and sign up thousands of customers was kind of a crazy thing for a few people sitting in an office at MIT. We had to work like maniacs and pull all kinds of crazy stunts to make that work, but that's how we work— we set huge goals." With his boyish smile, eyes ablaze with excitement, Lewin declared, "No matter what happens, we will not lose. We refuse to lose."

Although none of Akamai's executives, including Lewin, were the type to go out on the town, Las Vegas beckoned. Many enjoyed a few late nights, and two employees eloped. Then they all flew home and the work started all over again. And in the new climate of uncertainty, this meant working harder than ever before. It meant more business trips, more hours at the office. In short, it meant a lot of Akamai's employees were almost never at home. "I got sucked in, Danny got sucked in, and we both sucked each other in, and you never escape that," recalled Leighton. For some who had families, the absence of work-life balance began to take a toll. Spouses complained, relationships outside work fractured, and some couples split. "It's hard to stay married when you're in that life because you're working all the time, and when you're home you're still in work mode," said Earl Galleher, who left Akamai in early 2000. "But it was also so exciting, and we knew we were in this time that wouldn't last forever. Even in the moment, we'd say this may never happen again in our lifetimes, and we'd just go [on working]."

They could rationalize the grueling schedule with the promise of a big payout. But even life-altering economics wasn't enough to make some marriages work, including Lewin's. As a result, he and Anne separated temporarily, and he moved out of the family home. To many co-workers and friends, the fracturing of his relationship with Anne didn't come as a surprise. While he always counted her and the boys as his top priority, Lewin's primary commitment—for the better part of two years—had been Akamai. "No one was spending a ton of time with anyone outside the office—this was all we did," said Jonathan Seelig. "The company had an impact on everyone's personal lives."

In some ways, Lewin's flirtation with freedom could have been the result of losing his adolescence in an unwanted move to Israel. Friends say that, with no time to enjoy young adulthood—like summers spent at the beach or parties in college dorms—Lewin had an unsatisfied need to cut loose and enjoy his status as a high roller at the top of the boom. In July 2001, *Enterprise Systems* named him to its list of top ten leaders in technology, writing: "Lewin has the power to determine his company's future in what will likely be one of the most fiercely competitive IT markets over the next two years—content delivery. While a down economy has made companies reluctant to take on the expense of innovative technologies, analysts still see a huge market for solutions that speed the transmission of data over the Internet. If Lewin continues to drive innovation at Akamai, the Cambridge, Mass.-based firm could be in position to reap the profits when demand starts to pick up in this space."[1]

While Lewin never let his money inflate his ego, he did have a lot of it. In April 2001, *Forbes* magazine ranked him number 72 out of its "The 100 Highest Rollers"—an annual list of top-earning titans in high-tech, topped that year by Bill Gates. At age 30, Lewin's net worth was $285.9 million. Just below him was Leighton, 44, worth $284.3 million. The text read, "These guys [Leighton and Lewin] can freestyle algorithms in their sleep. Plus, Lewin's experience in the Israel Defense Forces should come in hand as the battle for Internet content delivery gets bloodier…"[2]

Lewin used some of his money to buy a new home, which he lived in for some time without Anne. It was a bachelor pad, outfitted with a hot tub and a Sony sound system. But Lewin also set up a room for Eitan and Itamar, his commitment to his sons unwavering. He hosted a few parties and bought a few more motorcycles—BMWs and Harleys. And, for a time, Lewin also started dating other women. The fact that Lewin strayed from Anne wasn't talked about much at Akamai. There was the occasional whisper; people had a sense of what was happening almost as soon as Anne stopped coming by. But there was too much pressure for anyone to really stop and judge. They were worried about their stock equity, their countless hours at the office, even the future of their jobs at Akamai.

Saving Akamai from the crash became so labor-intensive that Lewin didn't even have much time to enjoy his flirtation with a single life—or even a life of great wealth. By the spring of 2001, friends and family were having a hard time connecting with Lewin by cell or e-mail—he was always too busy. For the first time in years, Greenberg and Lewin went months without speaking. Sometime that spring, Lewin sent Greenberg a brief note saying he was sorry. "I've been a bad friend," he wrote. Greenberg didn't need an apology. He knew Lewin was fighting to keep Akamai, and his personal life, afloat.

By April, no measure of confidence could keep the feeble markets from taking a toll. The company carried out its first layoff, eliminating more than 180 jobs, or 14 percent of its work force. At the same time, Akamai warned that its revenue for the first quarter and the full year would fall well short of earlier expectations. In an official statement, the company said its business suffered because of general economic weakness as well as "continuing fallout among dot-com customers."[3]

Lewin was beginning to feel the strain, and upped the pressure on his staff. On May 8, at 10:30 p.m., he sent a four-page e-mail to his project management team. In it, he hammered home the belief that they needed to reassess their "leadership" roles for the company to make its goals of 150 new customers and an average $20K in monthly recurring revenue.

FROM: danny@akamai.com

Talking about how to lead people can be a little "cheesy" at times; however, in my experience you need to get over the discomfort and create a plan to lead—just like you would create any plan of action... There are a zillion things a great leader does to create and lead a team...I want to focus on the ones I believe are the most important. There are only three:

1. Lead by example
2. Suffer together
3. Hold people accountable and get rid of non-performers

If a team needs to work weekends to be successful—the leader will work weekends, holidays and nights.

In July, *Forbes* ran a story under the headline "Akamai's new Internet turbocharger saves Web sites money. Can it save Akamai, too?" It summed up Akamai's predicament well:

With Akamai stock down from $327 just 18 months ago to $7.60, Conrades badly needs this bet to pay off. Last quarter the company lost 150 dot-com customers, more than 10% of its base, with another 50 expected to drop away this quarter. Conrades has no margin for error. If EdgeSuite doesn't catch on, his firm will become yet another footnote in the history of dot-com madness.[4]

By summer 2001, Akamai's stock was so low (at $5) that Leighton recalled a conversation with Lewin in which they both thought how great it would be for it to go back up to at least $20. "Neither of us ever got really down. And the one percent of the time one of us did, the other would smack the other around a bit," said Leighton. "But the reality at that time was that things looked rough and we weren't going to escape it."

It might have been the fight to keep Akamai alive, or maybe it was just some strange, inexplicable combination of circumstances that collided sometime late that summer, but Lewin gained a much greater perspective on his life outside Akamai. First came a visit from his mother *and* father, the first one Charles had made since Danny, Anne, and the boys left Israel five years earlier. When asked why he didn't visit more often, Charles Lewin said very little, noting his decision was rooted in "principle." Friends of Danny's speculated that to leave Israel, to him, would be to leave the life he created for his family when he made the bold decision to make *aliyah*. He didn't want to endorse a life for Danny of some big-moneyed businessman, trapped in the culture of wealth that exploded in the dot-com boom. Of course, Peggy Lewin, who often visited Cambridge, disagreed, calling Charles' decision one made "out of stubbornness."

Danny had made several trips to Israel that year to see his family, but friends say he desperately wanted his father to come to Cambridge and see what he had built. He wanted him to be proud. Peggy didn't know exactly why Charles changed his mind. Nor, for that matter, did Charles. In the first week of September 2001, Charles and Peggy arrived in Boston for a long weekend. They toured Akamai, walked around Cambridge, and talked over a lot of what life had thrown at them over the course of five years. Looking back on the visit, Charles said, "Things occur that we don't understand in the usual frame of our understandings, and my going there was one of them." He added, "It was something *b'siyata dishmaya* [with the help of heaven]."

One evening during that same week, Lewin called Seelig, who was then living in the Back Bay neighborhood of Boston, and asked if he could drop by. It was late in the evening—sometime around 10:00 or 11:00 p.m.—but it had been months since Seelig had the opportunity to talk to Lewin outside of Akamai, so he welcomed him in. Over beers and a game of pool, Lewin and Seelig caught up on everything—work, life, family. Seelig recalled that Lewin seemed to have an unusual sense of peace about him. Lewin told Seelig that the visit from his parents, particularly the chance to see Charles in Cambridge, was monumental. He also told Seelig that he thought he'd figured out how to make his marriage work and that he wanted to spend more time with Anne and his sons. He stayed until past midnight, and when he left, Seelig had the distinct sense that something in Lewin had changed. "I remember him leaving and that I thought, 'That felt really good.'" Seelig noted. "He seemed so grounded and stable."

With more layoffs ahead, it was a terrible week for Akamai, but Lewin approached the tumult with his usual cheer and buoyancy. He was scared—the stock had plummeted and a few of Akamai's customers were on the verge of collapse—but he didn't show it. On September 10, Lewin called a meeting at Akamai for more than a dozen employees. In a conference room, Lewin offered up a new vision for the company, one that was clear and well planned. "Danny was very focused," observed Julia Austin, who was still in charge of the engineering team. "He told us that we were going to shift direction and talked about where we were going next as a company."

At the end of the meeting, which lasted well over eight hours, Austin and her co-workers—somewhat daunted by the task at hand—

tried to convince Lewin to change his plan to travel to Los Angeles the next day and stay in Cambridge to shepherd the layoffs and restructuring. Lewin opened his Blackberry and, for a moment, seemed to consider it, but then said he couldn't, adding "You guys will be fine."

Later that evening, Leighton and Lewin got together for the grim task of eliminating approximately 500 of the company's 1,500 employees. Both of them knew it was just the first round; by their estimates, Akamai would have to downsize at least 500 more for any chance of survival. Then they'd have to handle the issue of morale; they'd have to convince those who remained that the ship wasn't sinking. "I remember that night distinctly. It was a horrible, horrible night," Leighton said. "We recruited these people. They were our friends, and we'd all worked so hard together." Leighton said Lewin was emotionally drained by the layoffs. He'd personally hired so many staffers, and he agonized over the decision of whom to let go.

Leighton and Lewin worked through the night, and as the hours ticked by, they talked not just as business partners, but also as friends. "It had been an unusual week for Danny in some respects. A lot had transpired and he had definitely reached some closure on a bunch of issues related to his family," said Leighton. "It was good that he had that opportunity to have his parents visit and that his Dad was here. He had a sense of peace." Leighton also recalled Lewin talking about a motorcycle accident he'd had a few weeks earlier, when a car swerved and hit him, causing a minor injury to his shoulder. Lewin said that instead of approaching the driver and knocking him out, he realized he was in pain and that it would be better to just back off. "It was a surprising thing for him, because he was always on top as it were, and there was always this sense that no one could hurt him," said Leighton. "He did say that he'd come to grips with his own mortality in some sense."

It was not until 2:00 or 3:00 a.m. on September 10 that Lewin and Leighton wrapped up their work. Lewin had a flight to catch to California in just a few hours, so he said goodbye to Leighton. Late that night, Lewin chose to return to the home he shared with Anne and the boys. In the weeks prior to this, he and Anne had begun to reconcile, and just recently decided to give their marriage another chance. The two of them hoped, Anne said, to remain together for the rest of their lives.

E arly on the morning of September 11, 2001, Lewin kissed Anne goodbye and drove from his home to Boston's Logan International Airport. He arrived just in time to catch American Airlines Flight 11, scheduled for departure at 8:00 a.m. and bound, non-stop, for Los Angeles. It was a trip he had taken so many times—more than thirty in the past year—that he knew the flight crew by name, the numbers of the most comfortable seats, and the makes and models of the aircrafts. The plane was partially full—81 passengers, 9 crew members, and 2 pilots, Captain John Ogonowski and First Officer Thomas McGuinness.[5]

Like Lewin, many of the passengers seated in business class were traveling for work on the daily scheduled flight: a television producer, actress, photographer and several businessmen. But Lewin was a standout among them, dressed more like a college kid—in his Gap blue jeans, t-shirt, and grey Nike sneakers—than an Internet entrepreneur. Lewin settled into his seat, 9B, and pulled out his Blackberry to make a phone call before departure.[6] Co-workers say Lewin almost always made calls up until the moment one of the flight attendants reprimanded him for failing to shut down his device. Around 7:30 a.m., with the plane still sitting on the runway, he called Akamai's in-house attorney, David Judson. Lewin knew Judson was an early riser and often one of the first to arrive at the office. He wanted to check on some paperwork Judson had been preparing for an upcoming deal. Judson said Lewin sounded full of energy despite the sleepless night and looming layoffs. They spoke for about fifteen minutes, until Lewin abruptly ended the call in preparation for takeoff.

"I've gotta go," Lewin told Judson. "They're telling me I have to hang up my phone."

American Airlines Flight 11 took off from Logan on schedule at 7:59 a.m. The plane headed due west and held on course for sixteen minutes until it passed Worcester, Massachusetts. Then, instead of taking a southerly turn, it suddenly swung to the north. Just before 8:14 a.m. the plane failed to climb to its assigned cruising altitude of 29,000 feet.[7]

At this point, it's possible Lewin suspected—perhaps before anyone else on the flight—that something terrible was about to happen. Having trained in the IDF's most elite counter terrorism unit, he had learned to identify signs of attacks well before they were carried out. He also knew conversational Arabic, enough to have picked up on verbal cues if the five Middle Eastern passengers gave any.

Around 8:15 a.m. a bloody hijacking began on board. Five terrorists—all of them wielding box cutters and knives—rose from their seats in business class and began to threaten passengers and the crew. Most of what we know about the hijacking comes from reports by two flight attendants in the coach cabin, Betty Ong and Madeline "Amy" Sweeney, who calmly and courageously relayed details of the hijacking as it unfolded to authorities on the ground. At 8:19 a.m., Ong told flight control, "The cockpit is not answering, somebody's stabbed in business class—and I think there's Mace—that we can't breathe—I don't know, I think we're getting hijacked." In a separate call, Sweeney reported the plane had been hijacked and two flight attendants had been stabbed. Sweeney also confirmed that a passenger in business class had been stabbed to death, his throat slashed by one of the terrorists. The passenger, she said, was sitting in 9B—the seat assigned to Danny Lewin.[8]

Based on the evidence gathered from these phone calls and authorities on the ground, the 9/11 Commission Report concluded that, in those first twenty minutes of the flight, Mohamed Atta—the only terrorist on board trained to fly a jet—probably moved to the cockpit from his business-class seat (located within arm's reach of Lewin's seat), possibly accompanied by Abdulaziz al-Omari. As this was happening, according to the report, Lewin, who was seated in the row just behind Atta and Omari, was stabbed in the neck by one of the hijackers—probably Satam al-Suqami, who was seated directly behind Lewin, out of view.

Between 8:25 and 8:32, in accordance with the FAA protocol, Boston Center managers started notifying their chain of command that AA Flight 11 had been hijacked and was heading toward New York Center's airspace. At 8:44, Sweeney made her last call to ground control: "Something is wrong. We are in a rapid descent . . . We are flying low. We are flying very, very low. We are flying way too low."

Seconds later, Sweeney said, "Oh, my God, we are way too low." Silence.[9]

At 8:46 a.m., the Boeing 767 slammed into the North Tower of the World Trade Center, killing everyone on board.[10]

CHAPTER 11

Gutted

"One man's candle is light for many."

— TALMUD ON SHABBAT

In Boston that morning, the sky was the same deep, brilliant blue as it was across the Northeast, but the air felt slightly cooler, just bracing enough to carry with it the invigorating sense of possibility that comes with early autumn.

The day began like most at Akamai, with the staff trickling in around 8:30 a.m. Many people had recently returned from summer vacations and were still settling back into work. They were also adjusting to Akamai's new reality—a stock trading at around $3 a share, a shrinking customer base, and talk of impending layoffs. The mood was slightly quieter than usual, with Lewin, Leighton, and Conrades all out of the office. And those who had attended the lengthy meeting the day before were focused on carrying out a drastic shift in strategy.

Sometime before 9:00 a.m., the NOCC staff began to notice an unusual spike in Internet traffic, one that wasn't limited to one region or pathway. Someone checked the news and reported that a small plane had just crashed into the World Trade Center. No one was too alarmed, assuming that the accident involved a small aircraft that had veered off course. Within minutes, however, it became clear the news was much worse and much more personal than anyone could have imagined. Someone shouted out that a second plane had hit the towers, and at the same time, it seemed everyone's cell phones and desk phones began to ring.

One floor above the NOCC, David Judson was in his office working on the notes he and Lewin had discussed that morning. Around 9:30 a.m., he received a phone call from his wife, who alerted him to the developing news. At some point, Judson said, she

- 207 -

mentioned that the first hijacked flight had originated from Logan and that it was headed for Los Angeles. Judson said the second he heard this, he abruptly ended the call blurting out: "Oh, my God, I've gotta go. Danny was on that flight." Judson went straight to Sagan's office, just around the corner from his.

"Paul, Danny was on that flight," Judson said.

"Are you certain?" asked Sagan.

Judson recounted his conversation earlier that morning, and told Sagan that Lewin had called from the tarmac just as the flight was preparing for takeoff. Judson felt sickened.

He and Sagan wanted to hold out some hope, but they both knew there was no reason to. Lewin was on the flight, and Judson suddenly realized he was almost certainly the last person at Akamai to speak with him before he was killed. Sagan said his journalistic instinct—one sharpened over decades spent covering tragedy for broadcast news—kicked in almost instantly. Only this time, the tragedy was personal.

Oblivious, Leighton was working from home that morning, supervising some renovations to the house that he and Berger had long planned to carry out but seemed never to have the time for. He was also preparing for a new class at MIT, which he was scheduled to begin teaching the next day. When he heard the news that a plane had crashed into the World Trade Center, Leighton said he turned on the television. "I saw disaster unfolding," Leighton recalled. It wasn't until he heard a newscaster say that one of the hijacked flights had left Logan bound for Los Angeles that Leighton began to think about Lewin. "That's when I got that chill up my spine that you get when you know something might have happened," he said. "I thought, 'What if he's on that plane?' Then I thought, 'No, he can't be.'"

Leighton tried to contact the office, but by this time the phone lines were jammed and he couldn't reach anyone. So he got in the car and drove in. "You know it was one of those things where you have a feeling that's like a nightmare—no, this can't be real," he recalled. When Leighton arrived at Akamai, he saw Anne Lewin in the lobby, crying. "That's when I knew," he said.

It would be days before the airlines confirmed passenger manifests from the four hijacked flights, two of which originated from Logan. But for Lewin's family, friends, and co-workers, Lewin's phone call to Judson, combined with the widespread knowledge that he had been booked on the regularly scheduled flight to Los Angeles, was evidence enough to confirm their loss. By 10:00 a.m., the entire office was gripped by a collective state of shock and grief. No one knew what to do. They felt like they'd been gutted.

Outside of Akamai, an eerie silence had fallen over Cambridge as people retreated indoors, seeking safety amidst rumors of a possible attack on Boston. Government officials ordered the mandatory evacuation of several of the city's financial institutions, federal offices, and large residential buildings along the waterfront. Police and U.S. Marshals were dispatched to patrol the streets and maintain order as a mass exodus from the city began.[1] At Akamai, however, no more than a few people left the building. In part, they were paralyzed by anguish. But they were also watching traffic on the Internet escalate like never before. Between embraces and audible sobs, they stared in disbelief at the screens in the NOCC, which were lighting up with lines of traffic spanning the globe. The office phones reached a fever pitch; the Web sites of some of Akamai's biggest customers were buckling. With telecommunications failing and people around the world desperate for information about their loved ones, several of these customers—including the Red Cross, the Federal Bureau of Investigation and, in a tragic twist of irony, American Airlines—could not afford for Akamai to fail.

Someone at Akamai needed to take the reins. CEO George Conrades and CFO Tim Weller were out in California for meetings and could not be reached. Leighton was in what he called a state of shock, so devastated he was unable to think clearly. Sagan had no choice but to take charge. "That day, an inordinate amount of responsibility fell on my desk, and for me, it was horrible," he remembered.

That morning, time seemed to slow down and every second brought with it more bad news, heightened anxiety, and various, painful stages of grief. Fortunately, Sagan said, "I had total clarity about what needed to be done." He added, "There are these times in life, and 9/11 was one of them for me, when all the unimportant things disappear. I went into this zone, which some people may have interpreted as unfeeling, but for me, it was just about how do we get from A to B to C."

At some point, Sagan sent an e-mail to the entire company confirming what most of them already knew: Akamai had not only lost its visionary co-founder, it had lost its heart and soul.

Ever since the writing of his prize-winning master's thesis in 1998, Lewin had called attention to the unpredictable nature of news, foreseeing a time when technology rooted in his algorithms would have the power to keep the Internet alive under an extraordinary crush of traffic. On September 11, 2001, the day of Lewin's death, the Internet faced its greatest test ever as news of the attacks made its way around the world. Everyone at Akamai faced a stark choice: pause and grieve or press onward. The answer, Sagan said, was clear: "We had to do what Danny would do."

Through a fog of grief, engineers spent the entire day reconfiguring servers to build capacity on Web sites for news, aid, and security organizations. The sales team set up a phone chain to contact clients and inform them of the news, while at the same time assuring them that Akamai was committed to serving their traffic throughout the tragedy. "We immediately went into all-hands-on-deck mode," recalled Sef Kloninger, who was managing the company's engineering and service performance.

That day, almost every major new site used Akamai services, including ABC.com, *The Chicago Tribune*, CNN, MSNBC, *The New York Post*, and the *The Washington Post*. And many of them called the company for crisis management. A Web tech at MSNBC, which was still using FreeFlow, not EdgeSuite, called to say the site was going to have to strip its pages to the lightest possible load or risk crashing. Engineers at Akamai helped them install EdgeSuite, and by mid-day on 9/11, MSNBC was able to deliver rich content, including 12.5 million streams of video, with Akamai's help. At Washingtonpost.com, a similar scenario unfolded. During an average day, the site had been running about thirty percent of its content, primarily images and video, from Akamai servers. That day, the newspaper relied on Akamai to serve more than fifty percent of its traffic and keep it flowing smoothly.[2]

At CNN, engineers were scrambling to keep CNN.com online. Earlier in the year, with the presidential election and the AOL–Time-Warner merger complete, the CNN Internet team had decided that it had sufficient server and network capacity to bring back the traffic served by Akamai to its own data centers. But the spike on 9/11 proved to be the Web equivalent of a 100-year flood. As the world became aware of the news, traffic to the Web site was doubling every 7 minutes, and the usual procedures—reallocating servers from less busy sites and reducing the size and content on the homepage were not enough to stay ahead of the tide.

Between 9:00 a.m. and 11:00 a.m., the systems team increased the servers for CNN.com from 10 to 44, and reduced the homepage to a single headline and image. At that point, however the site's internal network itself began to fail under the strain. There were other obstacles to quick response—much of the management team, including Gassel, was in Northern Virginia at a company-wide conference, which was rapidly abandoned. Others were in New York or still at home. With phone lines busy and networks jammed, communications were difficult and systems monitoring flaky.[3]

After additional attempts to relieve the network load, CNN reached out to Akamai, tested the old configurations, and by 1:30 p.m., Akamai was once again serving CNN's images. The site soon stabilized enough to return to a "light" but informative homepage.[4]

During that early afternoon lull, Gassel sent an email to Sagan and Lewin, thanking them for Akamai's help. Sagan replied, and informed Gassel that Lewin had been killed. Gassel recalls that "until that point I had been entirely focused on trying to keep the network running. The loss of Danny, who had become a friend, suddenly made the events of the day both real and personal."

Knowing that there would be a heavy load for several days, over the rest of the afternoon and evening CNN staff continued to redeploy servers, and AOL engineering contributed 108 newly arrived servers of their own. Total Traffic on 9/12 was double that of 9/11, and CNN would run in this configuration for another two months.

Web traffic for Akamai's global network of clients, including the major news media sites, surged by a factor of five throughout the day. Akamai managed the crush, serving more than 1,000 billion hits and 150 million video streams related to the catastrophe. "September Eleventh was a day that proved everything

Danny was saying—that this could be done, that this will work," Leighton said.

"It was surreal," declared Seelig, who recalled working about eighteen hours straight after learning of Lewin's death. "In one day, Akamai went from the depths of despair to demonstrating to the world that we could do all the things we had promised. And then some. That's because of what Danny built."

At about 5:00 p.m., Sagan sent an e-mail to the company thanking everyone for their work. The Internet withstood its most titanic test ever, he wrote, and Lewin would be proud.

In Israel, around 10:00 a.m. Tuesday morning on September 11, hours before Lewin had boarded his flight in Boston, Peggy and Charles Lewin landed at Ben Gurion airport in Tel Aviv, tired but invigorated by the visit with Danny, Anne, and the two boys.

Around 4:00 p.m. that day, Peggy, who was at work, said Charles came into her office, located above their apartment, to tell her about an airplane smashing into the World Trade Center. Confused about the time and date, Peggy said at first she wasn't concerned. Thinking it was Monday, September 10, she assured Charles that Danny wasn't traveling. Soon after, the phone rang. It was Anne, calling to say she was certain that Danny was on Flight 11, and that he had been killed.

Devastated, the Lewins gathered to sit *shiva* (the Hebrew grieving period of seven days). It would be months before they had any concrete details of what happened on that flight, but they didn't need them. They knew that Danny would have never, ever gone down without a fight.

Although no flights were allowed out of, or into, the U.S. at the time, the Lewins reached out to El Al, the Israeli airlines, to ask if they could get on the first allowed flight bound for America to mourn the loss of their son, one of just five Israelis killed in the attacks. Three days later, U.S. authorities gave El Al permission to fly from Tel Aviv to John F. Kennedy Airport in New York. Thousands of people were clamoring to get on the flight, the first allowed into U.S. air space since the attacks. Officials at El Al later said they saved four seats for the Lewins the moment the family called to report the loss of Danny.

On September 14, they arrived in New York and took a taxi all the way to Brookline to be with Anne, Itamar, and Eitan. Michael Lewin recalled the streets having so much traffic that the driver sped off in the emergency lanes to get the grieving family to the Boston suburb as quickly as possible. They stayed for just over a week, long enough to sit *shiva* with Anne and the boys, and to attend a memorial service for Danny held, fittingly, at MIT's Kresge Auditorium on September 20, 2001.

Epilogue

When they look back on those days, everyone at Akamai agrees they were some of the darkest of their lives. The loss was too searing, the irony too thick. The remainder of 2001, to most of them, was a blur. They came to work and continued to carry out the company's new strategy. But they did it all weighted down by heartache. One of Lewin's coworkers said it was like running in snow—they kept moving, but every step felt labored. When they tried to look forward, they did so through the thick haze of grief. They saw nothing but the abyss left by Danny's absence.

But months passed, and with time, emotional strength regenerated enough for everyone at Akamai to realize that they had one last fight left in them, one that had to be waged in Lewin's honor. They knew it was going to be a fierce one. Although Akamai made it through the days and weeks immediately following the attacks, the company's financial problems were mounting. The attacks sent the U.S. economy further into the black, eating into Akamai's revenues and spawning widespread fears of a recession. Investors lost confidence in Akamai, fearing that Lewin's death meant death for the company.

Conrades recalled making rounds at the office to check in with staffers who "looked at me like deer in the headlights." As Conrades explained, "This was not the exuberant Akamai they were used to." Conrades became well versed at pep talks. "I'd say our stock is coming down, but we're still about one big idea," he recalled, also saying, "The technology still works. The business model works. Then I'd ask them: Do you still have bragging rights at the bar? The answer was yes, so I told them to have faith." He also told them, repeatedly, to do it for Danny.

Conrades made a pledge to Akamai's board that he would not step down until the company achieved sustained profitability. But in the two years following 9/11, Akamai was written off as another casualty of the dot-com boom. "Everybody had left us for dead," Leighton said. "We were gonna go broke. It was really that bad." The fall was precipitous. Once the stuff of legend, Akamai's stock was delisted by the NASDAQ after it fell below $1. The company's customers were going out of business faster than the sales representatives could close accounts. More downsizing was necessary, including most of the sales force. Conrades, Sagan and Leighton began citing a metric they called "quarters to live," guessing how many more quarters Akamai could stay in business.[1] But they kept pushing. Every time they thought about Lewin, they became resolute in their pledge never to give up. "The people were really good people, the technology was good, and you know, we were relentless," said Leighton. "It was all about Danny. He had instilled such a culture through the powerfulness of his personality and the people that he vetted and selected that everyone wanted to double down and work extra hard to make Akamai successful. We wanted to make it happen for him, and it was very, very hard."

Fortunately, Lewin had left behind what Akamai called one "gift" for the company: EdgeSuite. Akamai positioned EdgeSuite as the ticket to its comeback, one that would take the company beyond content delivery to content assembly, presentation, and delivery. Akamai, Conrades said, used EdgeSuite to form a new strategy akin to what Federal Express accomplished when it moved beyond the shipment of packages into the additional services of packing and preparing them for shipment. With EdgeSuite as the centerpiece of a new business plan, Akamai offered customers technology that would accelerate the movement of dynamic content—things like stock quotes, airline prices, auction listings, and weather reports. Prior to EdgeSuite, Akamai was delivering static pages, which were assembled before delivery, meaning everyone who clicked on them saw the same thing. Dynamic Web sites, in contrast, are put together on the spot and change frequently, often with every click—and EdgeSuite could do this very, very well.[2]

Lewin had pushed EdgeSuite onto the market in early 2001, putting his stamp on the new technology, which he predicted would be a winner. Lewin was right. The EdgeSuite service won over one hundred new customers by the end of 2001, and over half of them were entirely new to Akamai, including Novartis, Coca-Cola, and Saatchi & Saatchi. Existing customers like Apple also seized on EdgeSuite, adapting it for the 2003 launch of its hugely successful online music store, iTunes. By 2004, Akamai posted its first annual profit. The company has been profitable every year since, a leader not only in content delivery, but also in cyber-security. In 2003, Tom Leighton joined the President's Information Technology Advisory Committee (PITAC) and has since become a vocal advocate for more research into the prevention of online attacks, which he says pose a grave threat to personal, corporate and national security.

In July 2004, Lewin's remains were identified in the wreckage of the World Trade Center. He was buried at Sharon Memorial Park outside Boston.

That same year, the 9/11 Commission released its final report on the attacks. The section about Flight 11 clarified the release of fragmented and conflicting information in the wake of the attacks, some of it relating to Lewin's actions that day. An executive summary mistakenly leaked by the Federal Aviation Administration to the press stated that terrorist Satam al-Suqami shot and killed Lewin with a single bullet around 9:20 a.m. (obviously a typo, as the plane crashed at 8:46 a.m.). But almost as soon as the memo was leaked, FAA officials claimed it was written in error, and that Lewin was more than likely stabbed, not shot. The 9/11 Commission concurred, offering a more detailed summary: based on dozens of interviews with those who spoke with flight attendants Sweeney and Ong, the commission determined that al-Suqami most likely killed Lewin by slashing him in the throat from behind as he attempted to stop the hijacking. The time of his death was reported to be somewhere between 8:15 and 8:20 a.m., which—if fact—would make Lewin the first victim of the 9/11 attacks.[3]

The 9/11 Commission's final report did not state with certainty that Lewin single-handedly fought the terrorists, saying: "Lewin *may* have tried to stop the attacks." But no one who actually knew Lewin has a shred of doubt. In over one hundred interviews conducted with Lewin's friends and family in the creation of this book, every subject interviewed said there was no way Lewin could have sat idly by and watched terrorists hurt flight attendants and attempt to hijack the plane. Most people said they knew he'd been heroic the moment they heard he was on the flight, and that they could write their own narrative based on what they knew of Lewin's physical strength, counterterrorism training, and fighting spirit. Lior Netzer, who served with Lewin in the army and later worked with him at Akamai, said they had been trained to turn on their own aggressiveness like a light switch at the first sign of trouble. "The minute you hear a gunshot you go into aggressive mode," explained Netzer. "Particularly in dealing with counterterrorism."

"I know Danny fought back," said Greenberg. "Knowing his character and his training, we know that he got up and tried to do something, and I think he might have taken one of those thugs down with him. I know, beyond a doubt." When Greenberg spoke at Lewin's memorial, he called him "the first victim of the first war of the twenty-first century."

On the tenth anniversary of 9/11, several hundred friends and coworkers gathered at Akamai's headquarters in Cambridge to remember Lewin. Dressed in black from head to toe, Leighton stood on a patch of grass in the courtyard outside the building and paid tribute to his friend. Voice wavering, he told the crowd that Lewin was a hero, and that his legacy continues to inspire him, and everyone at Akamai, to this day. Leighton dedicated a small apple tree in the courtyard to Lewin, formally unveiling a plaque in his memory at its base.

That same day in Israel, the Jewish National Fund and the Jerusalem Municipality held a service at the country's memorial—the largest to 9/11 outside the U.S.—honoring the five Israelis lost in the attacks, including Lewin. Peggy, Charles, Jonathan, and Michael attended. Situated at a scenic, peaceful spot tucked away in the Jerusalem Forest, the memorial can only be reached by a narrow, winding road through the trees. Prime Minister Binyamin Netanyahu spoke, in addition to Jerusalem Mayor Nir Barkat. Barkat, who met Lewin in the late '90s at a meeting for tech entrepreneurs in Cambridge, said he considers Lewin an Israeli hero: "It took a while for us to learn that Danny had retaliated—he tried to save that plane," Barkat said. "He excelled at everything he did; he was willing to take risks, and unfortunately, he lost his life when he took one."

Peggy and Charles still live in Israel in French Hill, in the same neighborhood they settled in with their three young boys in 1984. In 2002, an agent from the FBI paid them a visit, sharing the chilling recordings and transcripts from the flight attendants as evidence that Danny had been killed in some sort of struggle with the terrorists. They said the meeting brought them comfort and closure; it was an official acknowledgement of what they already knew. Peggy is still a practicing pediatrician, one of the most popular in Jerusalem. Charles is retired and continues to write poetry, which he publishes under the pen name Yaakov Ben David. Much of it contains references to the loss of his son and the violence of 9/11. Michael and Jonathan are both successful technologists and businessmen, each with their own large families in which the legend of Danny lives large. The family gathers every anniversary of 9/11 to remember Danny. Charles said he prays for him every day, multiple times. To honor Danny's memory, the family supports the work of MEMRI, the Middle East Media Research Institute.

Anne Lewin eventually remarried and had another child—a girl. She still lives in Brookline. Anne has never spoken publicly about the loss of her husband. Today she can only say that she still misses him terribly, and wishes their love story had not come to such a tragic end. Eitan and Itamar—who were four and eight, respectively, at the time of Danny's death—have grown into teenagers, and friends say they are, in many ways, spitting images of their father.

Marco Greenberg said he thinks of Lewin every day. After 9/11, he realized Flight 11 had flown almost directly over his home in Great Barrington, Massachusetts, just before Lewin's murder. In 2005, Greenberg moved with his wife, Stacey, and kids to Boston from New York to try and restart his career and settle somewhere new. Instead, he said, he ended up feeling emptier than ever. He moved back to New York, only then realizing he moved not for a change, but to look for his friend. It was then that it finally hit him that Lewin was gone. In a file cabinet, Greenberg keeps an envelope filled with snapshots that illustrate their friendship and a small patch from Lewin's army uniform, an insignia with several blue bars that Lewin gave to him when he left Israel for MIT. "I wouldn't have anything without Danny," he said. "But I'd give it all back to see him again." Greenberg has worked tirelessly to keep Danny's memory alive, including the creation of an annual writing award—on the topic of technology and cyber-terrorism—in Danny's name at the U.S Army War College in Carlisle, P.A.

Those who knew Lewin personally are dwindling at Akamai, but the company keeps his legacy alive with its annual "Danny Lewin Award" for excellence, given out to employees considered "titans" as once defined by Lewin as the very best. Its first winner was Mike Afergan, the Harvard student to whom Lewin once turned for the entire Apple project. Afergan is now a senior vice president. In Lewin's name, many friends and coworkers continue to support the Akamai Foundation, the company's charitable organization promoting math education and the next generation of technology entrepreneurs.

A block away from the office, near the MIT computer labs where Lewin and Leighton worked out their early algorithms, the intersection of Main Street and Vassar Street was named Danny Lewin Square by the City of Cambridge to mark the first anniversary of the 9/11 attacks.

At the time of this book's publication, Akamai has offices around the world, more than 3,500 employees, and a market capitalization of $6.9 billion. In 2012, the company purchased the Israeli company Cotendo, one of its largest competitors, in a deal valued at approximately $268 million. With the acquisition, Akamai finally realized Lewin's dream of a presence in Israel. That same year, Leighton visited the Technion in Haifa, Lewin's alma mater. With the help of Professor Freddy Bruckstein, who first realized Lewin's genius in an academic setting, Leighton gave a lecture at the Computer

Engineering Center in Lewin's honor. When one of the young students asked how, through tempestuous market swings and the breakneck pace of emerging technology, Akamai has managed to succeed, Leighton barely hesitated: "One word, really," he said. "Danny."

Today, even as Akamai regularly controls between 15 and 30 percent of the world's Internet traffic, the company is not a household name. And it may never be, in part because Akamai remains the invisible layer—what Leighton still calls "the magic"—underlying the speed and security of the Internet as we know it. "A lot of times, when you log on and visit a Web site, you're actually visiting Akamai," Leighton said. Stealthily, but powerfully, Akamai delivers content for Apple's iTunes, Facebook, and Twitter, to name a few.

Akamai's core technology still relies on Lewin and Leighton's original algorithms. For this reason, TOC (the theory group at MIT) enjoys a much higher profile today. The same is true for the theory departments at top research universities around the country. And the algorithm, though still elusive and abstract, is widely appreciated and admired as all-powerful in the world of technology. Algorithms are not only the driving force behind Akamai; they are the invisible force behind Apple's music recommendations, Amazon's pricing and Google's search function.

Those who knew Lewin well, over a decade later, still marvel at the life of the friend they knew. When they imagine hearing Lewin's voice, he is almost always telling them "You're behind!" They agree, and they work harder because of it. When they ask themselves what could have been, they become overwhelmed with possibilities. Lewin, they say, could have easily become a tenured professor. His dream was to return to MIT, and he had plans to re-enroll for his PhD. Before his death, he became interested in the subject of infinity, which was fitting for someone who seemed to know no bounds. His family is certain he would have returned to Israel, where he could have been Prime Minister someday, another dream he harbored. But Lewin wanted to do so much, and had what it took to do it all, that there never would have been enough time for him.

In December 2012, Leighton became Akamai's new CEO, replacing Paul Sagan, who had been CEO since 2005. On whether he thinks Danny would be proud, Leighton is quick to credit his co-founder and best friend. "I think Danny would have been CEO," he said. Leighton sometimes marvels at Lewin's legacy, which he's seen as far as Bangalore, India, where a giant, smiling photograph of Lewin and Leighton covers a wall of Akamai's office there. "No one there knew Danny, but the work attitude and spirit they embody there is so much like his," Leighton said.

Leighton said he thinks often about Lewin, but no longer in the context of Akamai. Over time, he said, the feeling that Danny might charge into the room—smiling and wild-eyed with a big new idea—has faded. When he does think of Lewin, Leighton often recalls the time when they could talk for hours about their shared dream of proving mathematical theorems for a living. It was the moment in time before they took what they both knew, as theoreticians, to be a rare chance.

Leighton is no longer teaching at MIT; he's currently on leave, and said that for the foreseeable future he will be too busy running Akamai to return to the classroom.

One day, however, Leighton said he's likely to retire and become Professor Emeritus, allowing him to teach again. Academia is his lifeblood, after all, and it's where he first fanned the spark of the bright, indomitable young student who became his business partner and his best friend.

Acknowledgments

The reporting and writing of this book would not have been possible without the guidance, encouragement, and trust of many people—from those who patiently walked me through the complex worlds of theoretical computer science, content delivery networks, and the Israeli Special Forces, to my talented editors and the friends and family who offered me their unfailing support.

For entrusting me with the story of his lifelong best friend, I thank Marco Greenberg. Marco has undertaken numerous efforts to keep Danny's legacy alive, and when I set out to write this book he cheered me on at every turn, always repeating his conviction that Danny would want his story to be told. Marco also spent countless hours sharing memories and mementos of his friendship, details that no amount of reporting could have unearthed.

My sincere thanks also goes to Tom Leighton, Danny's best friend, mentor at MIT, and Akamai co-founder, for generously making the time for several lengthy interviews. Although he was promoted to CEO of Akamai during the writing of this book, Tom proved ever the gracious professor in his willingness to walk a journalist with limited schooling in the sciences through basic concepts in theory and computing. Tom's wife, Bonnie Berger, was also giving of her time, drawing on her recollections of Danny and Tom's extraordinary journey from MIT to Akamai.

To the Lewin family—Peggy, Charles, Michael, and Jonathan—I am most grateful. When I first contacted them in late 2011 (after an introduction by Marco Greenberg) to explain that I planned to write a book about Danny, the Lewins kindly agreed to a meeting with me. I traveled from New Jersey to Jerusalem without knowing what, exactly, they would be comfortable sharing. But they warmly welcomed me into their home, and spent a long evening reminiscing about the life, and loss, of their son and brother.

Thank you also to Anne Lewin Arundale. Although she did not make herself available for interviews for this book, Anne was willing to contribute a few significant details to the story, and generously allowed for the publication of several family photographs.

To Michael Salort, I owe a heartfelt expression of gratitude for first calling on me to help produce a documentary film about Danny, which we screened in a private tribute held at Akamai on the tenth anniversary of 9/11. Mike's unflagging belief in the beauty of Danny's story and my ability to tell it helped me through the more challenging moments of my reporting and writing.

For the facts and colorful anecdotes I needed to chronicle Akamai's beginnings and wild ride through the dot-com boom and bust I credit several current and former employees of the company, all of whom agreed to interviews in the interest of expanding Danny's legacy. In particular I thank Paul Sagan, who recounted stories in the kind of detail that only a former newsman could. Paul also responded, always promptly and good-naturedly, to my many emails filled with follow-up questions.

Jeff Young, who heads Akamai's media relations, helped a great deal in my reporting of company milestones, clarifying seemingly conflicting facts and tracking down the company's archival photographs and press material. George Conrades shared stories about Danny with the perspective of a seasoned executive who also loved speed. Laura Malo and Nancy Henry kindly managed all my queries for interviews with Akamai executives. Laura also dug up old photographs and many stories of her own.

John Sconyers always made himself available to answer my queries about Akamai's first customers and the race to sign them up. Melanie Wynkoop candidly recalled the exhilarating, exhausting buzz at the company before and after its IPO and the intensity of working with Danny. Mike Afergan vividly recalled the story of his first day of work, when Danny assigned him to spearhead a major project with Apple. Lior Netzer gave much of his time to interviews, thoughtfully expounding on Danny's character not only as a co-worker, but also as a proud Israeli and soldier in the elite unit of Sayeret Matkal.

Thanks also to David Judson, who agreed to a difficult interview in which he detailed his conversation with Danny on the morning of 9/11, less than an hour before he was killed on American Airlines Flight 11.

I'm grateful to the many former employees of Akamai who gave willingly of their time for this book, beginning with Jonathan Seelig. Jonathan was the first to explain the dizzying concept of consistent hashing to me on a whiteboard, which required a good deal of patience. Jonathan also endured a few lengthy interviews, and spoke freely of his friendship with Danny, which formed before the legendary 50K competition at MIT.

Earl Galleher carved out the hours for interviews in both Cambridge and Washington, D.C., and served up some of the most entertaining anecdotes for inclusion in the book. With his characteristic humor and candor, Earl described the early days at Akamai with much-appreciated flare, summing the time up with words that stuck with me: "We just knew we'd never have another experience like that."

I'm also grateful to Julia Austin, who shared her experience as one of the few female employees of Akamai to have worked directly and regularly with Danny, often clashing with him, but also admiring him greatly and appreciating his friendship. And to Will Koffel, Yoav Yerushalmi, Sef Kloninger, Bill Bogstad and Randall Kaplan—all of whom provided colorful details about their experience at Akamai.

There were many people who worked directly with Danny whose memories and thoughts informed this book. They include Art Bilger at Shelter Capital Partners, Todd Dagres at Spark Capital, Glenn Kaino at OWN and Gil Friesen, the legendary entertainment executive, who sadly passed away before the completion of this book.

Some of Akamai's early customers gave me invaluable details about how Danny and other company executives won them over, including Randy Dragon (Disney), David Filo (Yahoo), Sam Gassel (CNN), Farzod Nazem (Yahoo), Sean Moriarity (Ticketmaster), and Eric Schvimmer (The Washington Post). I am especially grateful to Sam Gassel, who painstakingly recalled the crush of Web traffic on 9/11, when CNN's

Internet operations had to rely heavily on Akamai to deliver news of the tragedy worldwide.

And I am hugely indebted to Dwight Gibbs, formerly of The Motley Fool. Dwight dropped everything to reminisce about Danny, ending many of our long interviews—after which I apologized for taking up so much of his time—with the heartfelt statement: "Anything for Danny." Dwight also helped me explain, in layman's terms, exactly how the Internet works—stripping some of my early drafts of unnecessarily complex detail.

Chris Pasko at Blackstone Advisory Partners walked me through every step of Akamai's historic IPO, which he led for Morgan Stanley. Chris kindly offered to read a few early drafts of this chapter of the story, which he edited with much thought and precision.

For taking me back to the atmosphere at MIT's renowned Lab for Computer Science in the mid-90s—specifically to the Theory group class of 1996—I credit Be Blackburn, Yevgeniy Dodis, Eric Lehman, Anna Lysyanskaya, Rina Pinagrahy, Amit Sahai and Salil Vadhan. Thanks also to Mark Gorenberg of Hummer Winblad Venture Partners, who shared his recollections of Akamai's performance at the 50K competition.

In Israel, in addition to the Lewin family, I am indebted to Professor Freddy Bruckstein at the Technion. More than two decades after Danny began classes at the university in Haifa, Freddy remembered Danny as a student and friend. Freddy was also kind enough to introduce me to Haifa; I'll never forget the sunset over Mount Carmel. I also thank Dan Perry at the Associated Press and Stephen Miller in the office of Jerusalem Mayor Nir Barkat, who both greeted me in Israel and helped me to map out my travel there. And a sincere expression of gratitude to Mayor Barkat, who took time out of his demanding schedule to share his thoughts on Danny's Israeli spirit, entrepreneurism and heroism on 9/11.

Also helping me to refine and insert detail into a story that transpired more than a decade ago were several of Danny's former co-workers at IBM's Research Lab in Haifa and friends/acquaintances in Israel, including (in alphabetical order) Roni El-Bahar, Orli Gann, Yuval Ishai, Moshe Levingale, Dean Lorenz, Ziv Maniawski, Brad Rephen, Meir Samson, Ronen Sarig and Shmuel Ur.

The creation of any book, of course, is a process—at times a highly collaborative one. I could not have seen this story to print without the help and expertise of several people, beginning with my agent, Nathaniel Jacks at Inkwell Management. Nat read one of my magazine features, tracked me down using social media, and asked me if I had any ideas for a book. Two years later, we have a book. Thank you, Nat, for pushing me to take the leap and write, and for diligently working to find a home for this story.

To everyone at my publisher, Da Capo Press, thank you, thank you... First to my editor, John Radziewicz, for his editorial wisdom and for the important, sage reminder that a great book is never really finished. To Jonathan Crowe, formerly of Da Capo, who enthusiastically supported my proposal from its inception. Also thanks to Fred Francis, Justin Lovell, Kevin Hanover, Sean Maher, and Kate Burke for serving as the force behind this book. Finally to freelance editor Marco Pavia, who stepped in during the last mile and shepherded the book, and the author, through the difficult final stretch with such good humor, encouragement, and patience. Mille grazie!

To the friends and extended family who expressed faith in me throughout the book-writing process, I am blessed and lucky to have you in my court. A special shout out to Jamie Stiehm, my dear friend and writing companion at the Georgetown Public Library, for a year of stellar support, counsel and brainstorming sessions over afternoon espressos.

I am also indebted to the discerning readers who bravely dove into a manuscript in the rough, taking the time to edit and share feedback. They include my mother, author Amy Knight, who caught errors even the best copyeditors could not have found at the last hour; Kari Niles, dear friend, talented writer and my arbiter of good literary taste; and veteran journalist and award-winning author Jim Wooten, who broke from his own writing to read my manuscript not just once, but three times, and offer invaluable feedback and encouragement.

A gesture of thanks also to research assistant Jasmine Adams at Georgetown University, and to Dan Monken at the US Army War College for inviting me to speak at the awards event in Danny's honor.

For never failing to communicate the sentiment that my successes are also theirs, I thank my parents, Malcolm and Amy Knight. While raising three spirited girls my Mom managed to write five books, and my Dad traveled to and worked in what seemed like every corner of the world.

I'm still not sure how they did it, but I know they proved to me that anything is possible with drive, curiosity and passion. I also owe a lot to my sisters, Diana and Allie Knight, for their support. Diana, thank you for accompanying me on a whirlwind, unforgettable reporting trip to Israel. And to my amazing extended family—Maggie and Buzz, who swept in during my absences and long work hours to help run the ship at home and care for our little girls. I could not have done this without your unflagging love and support.

For making this book possible, I thank my husband and best friend, Matt Raskin, for his tireless support of all my creative endeavors. During every stage of the book-writing process he stuck with me, pushing me when I faltered and counseling me when I crashed. Thank you for believing in me, and for understanding better than anyone why it is I need to write. And, finally, to the sunshine in my life: Sophie and Claire. The two of you inspire me not only to be a better Mom, but also a better journalist and citizen of the world. This book is for you.

Notes

CHAPTER 1

1. Barry M. Leiner, Vinton G. Cerf, David D. Clark, Robert R. Kahn, Leonard Kleinrock, Daniel C. Lynch, Jon Postel, Lawrence G. Roberts, Stephen S. Wolff, *The Past and Future History of the Internet, Communications of the ACM*, February 1997, Vol. 40, No. 2.

2. Katie Hafner and Matthew Lyon, *Where Wizards Stay Up Late: The Origins of the Internet*, (New York, Simon & Schuster, 1996).

3. Charles Haddad, "Boston: City thrives on ideas. Education complex drives booming software, biotech industries," *The Atlanta Journal and Constitution*, High-Tech Hot Cities section, October 6, 1993.

4. Farhad Manjoo, "Jurassic Web: The Internet of 1996 is almost unrecognizable compared with what we have today," Slate, February 24, 2009.

5. Elizabeth Weise, "Is the Internet Poised to Collapse? Some Say Yes, Some Say No," Associated Press, October 9, 1999.

CHAPTER 2

1. Neal Sandler, "Ex-Monopoly Battles Competitors: Bezeq Israel Faces Realities of Market," *New York Times*. October 8, 1999.

2. David Ivanovich, "Residents Keep Watch for Terrorist Bombs," Associated Press, September 12, 1984. International News.

3. Rich Cohen, *Brotherhood of Warriors*. (New York: Harper Collins, 2009).

4. Rich Cohen, "Stealth Warriors," *Vanity Fair*, 496 (December, 2001): 284.

5. Samuel M. Katz, *The Elite: The True Story of Israel's Secret Counterterrorism Unit: The Most Deadly Fighting Force in the World*. (New York, Pocket Books, 1996).

6. "Israeli premier turns to former commando comrades for top government leadership positions," Associated Press. August 29, 2012.

7. Muki Betser, with Robert Rosenberg, *Secret Soldier: The True Life Story of Israel's Greatest Commando*, (New York, Atlantic Monthly Press, 1996).

8. Rich Cohen, "Stealth Warriors," *Vanity Fair*, 496 (December 2001): 284.

9. By Joshua Hammer, et al., "Will Israel Hit Back?" *Newsweek*, February 11, 1991.

10. Patrick Tyler, "US Tells of Retaliatory Plan the Israelis Abandoned," *New York Times*, March 7, 1991.

11. Dan Senor and Saul Singer, *Start-Up Nation* (New York: Hachette, 2009), 74.

CHAPTER 3

1. "The History of Computing at Princeton," Princeton University. http://www.princeton.edu/oit/about/history.

2. Bruce Arden, *What Can Be Automated? The Computer Science and Engineering Research Study* (Cambridge, MA: MIT Press, 1980).

3. J. M. Graetz, "The Origin of Spacewar," *Creative Computing* (August 1981), 56–67.

4. David Karger later came to appreciate consistent hashing, expanding on the idea with his own research and supervising a seminal paper on its merits (co-authored by Lewin, Lehman et al.): *Consistent Hashing and Random Trees: Distributed caching protocols for relieving hot spots on the World Wide Web.*

5. David Berlinski, *The Advent of the Algorithm: The 300-Year Journey from an Idea to the Computer* (Orlando, Florida: Mariner Books, 2001), xii.

6. F. Thomson Leighton, *On Theory* (Forthcoming).

7. Knuth, Donald Ervin. "The Art of Computer Programming (TAOCP)". Retrieved 2012-05-20.

CHAPTER 4

1. Leslie Walker, Business at Cyberspeed; Brainstorm Becomes Quick Internet Hit, *The Washington Post*, January 24, 1999, A01.

2. Marc Ballon, MIT Springboard Sends Internet Company Aloft, Inc.com, December, 1998, Pg. 23.

3. MIT 50 K Press Release, 1998, MIT Newsroom: http://mitsloan.mit.edu/newsroom/50k/50kfunfacts.php

4. Leslie Walker, Business at Cyberspeed, *Washington Post*, January 24, 1999, A01.

5. Daniel M. Lewin, *Consistent Hashing and Random Trees: Algorithms for Caching in Distributed Networks*, Department of Electrical Engineering and Computer Science, Massachusetts Institute of Technology, May 1998.

CHAPTER 5

1. United States Patent and Trade Office, Patent # US6108703 A, Inventors: Leighton, F. Thomson, Lewin, Daniel, Assignee: Massachusetts Institute of Technology, filed July 1998.

2. Jon Gertner, *The Idea Factory: Bell Labs and the Great Age of American Innovation*, (New York, Penguin Press, 2012).

CHAPTER 6

1. Bart Ziegler, Thomas E. Weber, and Michael W. Miller, "Starr Report Makes History And Marks Web's Emergence," *Wall Street Journal*, Monday, September 14, 1998.

2. David Kravets, "Starr Report Showcases Net's Speed: September 11, 1998," *Wired*, September 11, 2009.

3. "Exodus Communication Annual Report 1999," Internet Corporation for Assigned Names and Numbers, https://archive.icann.org/en/tlds/i1/REGOP/Exodus%20proposal.htm

4. Robert Lenzner, "Personality Change," *Forbes* (April 3, 2000): P074–P080.

CHAPTER 7

1. Akamai Press Release: http://www.akamai.com/html/about/press/relcascs/1999/press_011499.htmlhttp://www.akamai.com/html/about/press/releases/1999/press_011499.html

2. John F. Thorsberg, "Sports Sidelines: NCAA's March (Cyber) Madness," CBS Marketwatch, March 11, 1999.

3. Bob Longino, " 'Star Wars' Fans Turn to Web for Trailer," Cox News Service, March 11, 1999.

CHAPTER 8

1. Doreen Carvajal, "Amazon Surge May Reflect the New Math of the Internet," *New York Times*, January 11, 1999, Late Edition—Final.

2. John Cassidy, *Dot.Con: How America Lost its Mind and Money in the Internet Era* (New York: HarperCollins, 2002).

3. "IBM 650," Wikipedia, last modified February 26, 2013, http://en.wikipedia.org/wiki/IBM_650

4. Julie Pitta and Bruce Upbin, "The Dark Side of Options," *Forbes*, 163, no. 10 (May 17, 1999) 210–213.

5. Bradley Spirrison, "Akamai Uses Force to Raise $35M Round," *Private Equity Week*, May 24, 1999.

6. Suein Hwang, Rebecca Blumenstein, Ann Grimes and Andrea Petersen, "Digits," *The Wall Street Journal*, December 23, 1999. B, 6:1.

7. "1999 Internet Caching Report Reveals Strong Market Growth," *Emerging New Applications*, PR Newswire, August 17, 1999.

8. David Strom, "The Caching Question," *Internet World*, September 15, 1999

9. Andrew Pollack. "Web-Page Distribution Could Unclog Internet Traffic Jams," *New York Times,* April 26, 1999.

10. Nick Wingfield, "Sandpiper Aims to Prevent Event-Driven Web Pileups," *Wall Street Journal*, June 17, 1999, B10.

11. Adam L. Penenberg. "Speed Racer," *Forbes*, 164, no. 7 (September 20, 1999): 200–202.

12. Regina Joseph, "Aloha Akamai," *Forbes*, June 18, 1999.

13. "Apple and Akamai Reveal Apple Investment to Cement Strategic Agreement," Akamai, August 18, 1999, http://www.akamai.com/html/about/press/releases/1999/press_081899c.html. Press release.

14. David Frith, "Tuesday Jobs to get real in QuickTime," *Australian*, August 17, 1999.

15. Margo Lipschitz Sugarman, "The Brain that Beat the World Wide Wait," *Jerusalem Report*, July 5, 1999, 38.

16. Paul Spinard, *The New Cool: Akamai overcomes the Internet's hot spot problem*, WIRED, August 8, 1999.

CHAPTER 9

1. Akamai Technologies Inc., SEC filing form S-1/A, September 27, 1999. EDGAR online.

2. Pete Barlas, "This Year's Internet IPOs Want To Party Like 1999," *Investor's Business Daily* (Los Angeles, CA), January 12, 2000, A06.

3. IPO Monitor Investor's Business Daily.

4. Raymond Hennessey, "Akamai Illustrates the Brevity Of Web Start-Up-to-IPO Period," *The Wall Street Journal.* December 8, 1999. C, 28:1.

5. John Hechinger, "Akamai Technologies' Shares Increase More Than Fivefold in First Session," *Wall Street Journal*, November 1, 1999, B6.

6. Andrew Caffrey, "For Six Months, MIT Will Study The Stock Pages," *Wall Street Journal*, November 10, 1999, NE2.

7. Jon G. Auerbach and William M. Bulkeley, "MIT Professor Stands to Reap Windfall As Web Start-Up Akamai Goes Public," *Wall Street Journal*, October 26, 1999, B7.

8. "Akamai Doubles Customer Base to 200 in Six Weeks," *Business Wire*, January 5, 2000.

9. "Akamai Mulling R&D Here, Founder Said," *Haaretz*, December 3, 1999.

10. "The Year in the Markets," *New York Times*, January 3, 2000, 1999, C17. Highlights Section.

11. Tom Kirchofer, "Akamai To Buy InterVu for $2.8B," Associated Press, February 7, 2000.

12. Steve Young and Bruce Francis, "Akamai Buying InterVu," CNNFN.

13. Ron Insana, "George Conrades of Akamai Technologies Loses Almost $195 Million on Paper Today," CNBC News Transcripts, March 15, 2000, 6:30 p.m., Eastern Time. (73 words).

14. "Net Stocks: Net stocks continue their tumble," CBS.MarketWatch.com, CBS, April 11, 2000.

15. Business Week Investor, *How Lockups Can Leave You Out in the Cold*, September 17, 2000. Emily Burg, The Lowdown on Lockups, *The Silicon Investor*, April 4, 2000.

16. *Digital Jam*, CNNFN, July 24, 2000, 7:30 p.m., Eastern Time.

17. "Akamai Shares Slump," from *Bloomberg News*, *New York Times*, July 26, 2000, C4.

18. Bruce Francis and Steve Young with Andrew Barrett, "Tech Stock Analysis," *Digital Jam*, CNNFN, August 1, 2000, 7:30 p.m., Eastern Time.

19. Jack McCarthy, "Akamai Unveils Enhanced Internet Content Delivery Service," *Network World*, October 23, 2000.

20. Bambi Francisco, "Web Stocks in Final Fade Out," CBS.MarketWatch.com, CBS, December 29, 2000.

CHAPTER 10

1. *Business Wire,* July 26, 2001, Thursday Akamai CTO and Co-founder Daniel Lewin Named to Enterprise Systems Power 100

2. Clint Willis, "The 100 Highest Rollers," *Forbes*, April 2, 2001, 1-11.

3. Ted Griffith, "Akamai to Slash Jobs, Sees Revenue Shortfall," CBS MarketWatch.com, April 4, 2001.

4. Daniel Lyons, "Living on the Edge," *Forbes*, July 9, 2001, 134-136.

5. "Brief of Accident," National Transportation Safety Board (NTSB), File # 1965. www.ntsb.gov.

6. American Airlines Flight 11 Manifest, obtained by *The Boston Globe*, http://www.boston.com/news/packages/underattack/news/aa_flight_11_mainifest_popup.htm

7. Anthony Summers and Robbyn Swann, *The Eleventh Day, the Full Story of 9/11*, (New York, Ballentine Books, 2011).

8. "American Airlines Flight 11," CNN. May 16, 2008.

9. Federal Bureau of Investigation, 9/11 Investigation (PENTTBOM): A selection of audio recordings from the Federal Aviation Administration (F.A.A.), North American Aerospace Defense Command (Norad) and American Airlines from the morning of Sept. 11, 2001.

10. John Kifnew, "After the Attacks: American Flight 11; A Plane Left Boston and Skimmed Over River and Mountain in a Deadly Detour," *New York Times*, September 13, 2001, 20. http://www.9-11commission.gov/report/911Report. pdf

CHAPTER 11

1. Tom Benner, Boston Shuts Down As Precaution, *The Patriot Ledger*, September 11, 2001, A6.

2. Jennifer Mears, "Content Delivery Networks Carry the Heavy Load; News Sites Credit Akamai, Others with Keeping Sites Available after Sept. 11 Tragedy," *Network World*, September 24, 2001, Pg. 33.

3. National Research Council of the National Academies, "*The Internet Under Crisis Conditions, Learning from September 11,*" (Washington, DC, National Academies Press, 2007).

4. William LeFebvre, CNN Internet Technologies, CNN.com: Facing A World Crisis, http://www.tcsa.org/archive/lisa2001/cnn.txt.

EPILOGUE

1. Bridget Finn, *A Star Is Reborn: Former dotcom sensation Akamai has shaken off 9/11 and reemerged as one of tech's hottest properties*, Business2.com, July 2005.

2. Thomas R. Eisenmann, Akamai Technologies, Harvard Business School Case Study # 9-802-132, March 1, 2002.

3. Richard Sisk and Monique El-Faizy, First Victim Died a Hero on Flight 11: Ex-Israeli Commando Tried to Halt Unfolding Hijacking, *Daily News*, July 24, 2004, 7. Uri Dan and Adam Miller, 9/11's First Victim Finally ID'd, *The New York Post*, July 11, 2004, Metro; Pg. 13

Index